HOPE *for* TROUBLED MARRIAGES

Overcoming Common Problems & Major Difficulties

Everett L. Worthington, Jr.

PEOPLE HELPER BOOKS, GARY R. COLLINS, *series editor*

INTERVARSITY PRESS
DOWNERS GROVE, ILLINOIS 60515

InterVarsity Press® is the book-publishing division of InterVarsity Christian Fellowship®, a student movement active on campus at hundreds of universities, colleges and schools of nursing in the United States of America, and a member movement of the International Fellowship of Evangelical Students. For information about local and regional activities, write Public Relations Dept., InterVarsity Christian Fellowship, 6400 Schroeder Rd., P.O. Box 7895, Madison, WI 53707-7895.

All Scripture quotations, unless otherwise indicated, are from the New Revised Standard Version Bible, copyright © 1989 by the Division of Christian Education of the National Council of the Churches of Christ in the USA and used by permission.

ISBN 0-8308-1602-X

Printed in the United States of America ∞

Library of Congress Cataloging-in-Publication Data

Worthington, Everett L., 1946-
    Hope for troubled marriages: overcoming common problems & major
difficulties/Everett L. Worthington, Jr.
        p.   cm.
    Includes bibliographical references.
    ISBN 0-8308-1602-X
    1. Marriage—United States.   2. Communication in marriage—United
States.   3. Marriage—Religious aspects—Christianity.   I. Title.
HQ734.W944   1993
646.7'8—dc20   92-34567
                                                                     CIP

16	15	14	13	12	11	10	9	8	7	6	5	4	3	2	1
06	05	04	03	02	01	00	99	98	97	96	95	94	93		

To the Shermans—
faithful Christians and friends

Introduction

The theme of this book is simple to state: God is promarriage. He is the healer and sustainer of marriages. People can help or interfere with God's work in their lives. If your marriage needs improvement, it can be helped—if you work on it.

This theme, though simple, is not easy to carry out. Still, I'm convinced that when married partners work on their relationship, their marriage can improve. For nearly twenty years I have counseled married couples, prepared couples for marriage and helped happy couples enrich their marriages. I have seen great changes in the lives of couples who are committed to each other and committed to work on their marriages.

I have conducted research on marriage and family relationships for almost as long as I have counseled. From my studies and practice, I am convinced that people can learn principles about marriage and can effectively apply that learning in their own relationships.

In this book, you'll develop a vision of marriage as an institution and a vision for your own marriage. You'll tackle the typical problem areas in marriage. You'll be provided with a framework for understanding marriage, and you'll find many practical suggestions that you can use to improve your marriage. More important, though, your new framework of understanding will allow you to devise creative ways to defeat marriage blahs and blues. You can also use this book to help a friend through his or her marriage struggles.

Technique

The approach I recommend is based on principles drawn from cognitive-behavioral and family systems theories of marriage. Cognitive-behavioral theories help people to align their thinking with reality and choose behavior that is positive and productive. Cognitive-behavioral theories emphasize the responsibility of both partners to improve their marriage through better communication and problem solving. Family systems theories focus on patterns of communication and ways marriage partners share power. Family systems theories look at the marriage as a whole—a perspective that complements the individual focus of cognitive-behavioral theory.

My Christian values undergird my recommendations, for I have tried to make my approach consistent with scriptural principles. Many scriptural passages deal directly with marriage, yet Scripture is not a marriage self-help book. The Bible communicates truth about humanity's past, present and future relationship with the triune God. Throughout Scripture, marriage is used as a metaphor for our relationship with God, while our relationship with the Father, Jesus and the Holy Spirit simultaneously provides a vision for what earthly marriage can be. Recognizing the limitations of metaphors, I nonetheless draw on Scripture to provide crucial insights for improving your marriage.

I pray that God will use this book to help you improve your marriage and gain a greater understanding of the Christian's marriage to Jesus.

There are three main ideas in this book.

1. God is at work to build contented and committed marriages. He sometimes changes marriages miraculously, but usually he works through his body—believing Christians who wish to conform to his revealed will. Your part, then, is to maintain a prayerful attitude and submit your marriage-improvement efforts to the lordship of Jesus.

2. There are six major aspects of marriage that deserve our attention: confession and forgiveness, closeness, communication, conflict resolution, assigning proper responsibility, and commitment. As we examine each of these areas, think about whether you need to make changes to improve your relationship.

3. Your efforts to change will be most effective if you assess your

marriage and try to change the areas that need the most work. Thus, this book follows a *counseling approach* rather than an *advice approach*. Advice tends to be general—the same for everyone—while a counselor assesses your relationship carefully and tailors suggestions for change to your particular situation.

Further, the book's structure is based on respect for your time, energy and individuality. Most people are simply too busy to read an entire book if most of it doesn't apply to them. This book is structured so that you can read only the sections that address areas in which you assess yourself to be needy.

Read chapters one through five. Then read the *beginning* of each of the following chapters (chapters six through eleven). At the beginning of each chapter you will make a careful assessment of your marriage; if no action is needed, move on to the next chapter.

Reading selectively will help you be a good steward of your time. Remember, too, that reading with your spouse can be valuable. You may want to answer the marriage-assessment questions separately and then compare your answers. As you discuss the similarities and differences in your responses, you'll learn more about your marriage—and more about how to improve it.

1

A Positive
Vision of
Marriage

At marriage two people become one flesh. But sadly, this new flesh, this union, does not always thrive.

Even the healthiest flesh inevitably develops problems and becomes broken. When that flesh is made whole, it is God, the healer, who restores health. Sometimes we marvel at his providence in unilateral healing. At other times we serve as his means of healing.

This book is a practical guide for helping heal the fractures in your marriage, whether they are hairline fractures, simple breaks, or compound fractures that threaten the very life of the marriage. But good medicine is preventive as well as therapeutic. So this book not only will help heal your marriage's fractures but will also help prevent other complications. And your life as a couple will be deepened and enriched.

Before we get down to the practical suggestions for helping your marriage, we must consider your goal. In this first chapter I survey where many of our modern views of marriage come from. Then I outline a scriptural vision of marriage and, finally, tell you the framework I'll use to help you make your marriage better.

Media Images of Marriage

"Where there is no vision, the people perish" (Prov 29:18 KJV). At the heart of any marriage is a vision. In our media age, our pictures of marriage are often the products of the visual media. They may be caricatures of marriage as depicted in Gary Larson's clever "Far Side" cartoons, or they may reflect the constant marital conflicts of "Hagar" and "Andy Capp." The image may come from a television sitcom—"The Simpsons," "Family Ties," "Married . . . with Children"—in which wisecracking children are at odds with do-your-own-thing mothers and brainless fathers. Despite the vicious put-down humor, the family ends each thirty-minute episode in a blissful homeostasis with a promise to return next week for more painful laughs.

With the rising popularity of the home videocassette industry, one's primary vision of marriage might come from a movie. *On Golden Pond* might provide a cameo of an elderly couple. *Kramer Versus Kramer* may intrude into the fantasies of a young couple as they struggle to iron out the wrinkles of the first years of marriage. The image may be a "love-conquers-all" fairy tale, like *The Princess Bride,* promising in the end that the loving couple "lived happily ever after." With each passing year, more movie images of marriage glorify instant intimacy (love and devotion within the first day), microwave sexual encounters (hot and steamy within minutes), "fatal attractions," and complex emotional dilemmas that resolve nicely within two hours.

Visions are also forged through reading, conversation and private thought, yet we are becoming so overcommitted to career advancement and other activities that contemplative reflection has become scarcer in recent years.

Romantic Ideals

Despite the modern pressures that surge against us like ocean waves, most people *want* a more positive view of marriage than they can get from television or movies. We long for commitment and contentment, and we work to build long-lasting happiness. Our mental images of marriage are being pounded by the surf of modern values. But for

Christians they have not been completely eroded.

Scripture provides the rocklike foundation that can withstand the pounding tides. Unlike the sandy beach of twentieth-century values that will be washed away with twenty-first-century waves, Scripture is a sort of living reef that provides a haven for a variety of lives. The base of our culture, which resides in individuals' unconscious minds, is a Judeo-Christian heritage.

Mark and Cleo have the perfect Christian marriage. They share intimate walks around the block at least three times a week. They make love frequently, usually having simultaneous orgasms. They communicate regularly, often taking days off from work to drive to the mountains for romantic talks. When they disagree, they work out their differences without hurt, and on the rare occasions that a harsh word does escape their lips, they are quick to confess and forgive. They start each morning with prayer together and have family devotions each night around the dinner table with their six children.

Mark and Cleo don't exist. They are a romantic ideal of the Christian couple. Yet many people would like to have a marriage like Mark and Cleo's.

I play soccer in an adult league. Sometimes I visualize myself as Pelé or Diego Maradonna—dribbling like a comet, bobbing and weaving through the opposition to finish with a rocketlike shot past the goalie's futile lunge. But in a real-life soccer game, when those fantasies are fully in my mind, I usually feel muscles and tendons in my legs going "spronnng." My vision simply does not match reality, and because my vision is too ambitious, I overextend myself.

I believe that a vision of the "perfect" Christian marriage can be similarly harmful to the Christian couple. Of course we should have a positive vision of marriage, but a romantic ideal leads to the disappointment of unfulfilled expectations. A real-life marriage will rarely measure up to the perfect fantasy.

The vision of marriage derived from Scripture is not a romantic ideal. It is a flexible structure that molds to a couple rather than a one-size-fits-all plastic mold into which all couples must fit. Let's examine this scriptural perspective to fortify a positive vision for marriage.

Marriage Reveals Our Relationship with God

Marriage is spiritually intimate. When two people marry, God mystically joins their spirits. The effects of this union are not always apparent to us, because the joining is spiritual. For example, Paul, in discussing marriage between believers and unbelievers, recommends that such mismatched spouses should not divorce if the unbelieving spouse is willing to stay. He says that "the unbelieving husband is made holy through his wife, and the unbelieving wife is made holy through her husband" (1 Cor 7:14). In some mysterious but powerful way, marriage sanctifies both spouses in God's eyes.

Marriage is intended to be an intimate blending of personalities. My heart and lungs are clearly different organs, but they must cooperate to make my body function. When I have a respiratory infection, the heart pumps early-warning cells and killer cells through the bloodstream to the site of the infection, then removes the debris of microbiological war. Heart and lung work in harmony, ensuring oxygenation of the blood to nourish the brain and body. By God's design, heart and lung do not try to perform each other's functions.

Similarly, God has designed marriage partners to operate in intimate cooperation. Spouses' functions are intertwined, and their personalities, troubles and triumphs affect each other. Couples operate on a principle called *reciprocity.* When partners compliment, praise, share affection with, laugh with and communicate with each other, they reap returns in kind. When partners put down, criticize, ignore or argue with each other, those poisons are likewise returned in kind.

Marriage is a continual dance of separation and union. Partners come together sexually and then move apart. They experience times of emotional closeness and times of distance. The couple twirls, locked in each other's embrace, then spins away to arm's length, only to glide back together.

This graceful waltz parallels our relationship with God through Jesus. We embrace the Lord on one beat and at the next seemingly want to break free. We go our way, but we hold desperately to his hand and long for the reunion. We experience both unity and individualism in this ever-changing intimacy.

Marriage is intended to be permanent. Based on covenant, marriage is an agreement symbolizing the sacrificial death of individual will in service of the other person. In ancient days, a covenant was sealed when two people killed an animal, split its body and walked together between the halves. Our modern marriage ceremony is reminiscent of this covenantal tradition when the bride and groom walk the aisle between their family members.

God's institution of marriage is meant to remind us continually of his covenants with his people. His covenant with Abraham—the old covenant—was sealed with animal blood and guaranteed God's fidelity to provide for Abraham's descendants. God's covenant with Christians, the new covenant, was sealed with Jesus' blood and guaranteed God's fidelity to provide for believers. Marriage, our covenant with a mate under God's care, is intended to be a model of fidelity in which spouses provide for each other. God intends the marriage covenant to be permanent (Mal 2:14-16; Mt 5:31-32; Mk 10:2-12; Lk 16:18; 1 Cor 7:10-11).

Marriage is a mystery. God has instituted marriage for his own purposes, which we cannot fully understand. We can say, however, that marriage serves two spiritual purposes. It helps us (1) transcend our own self-centeredness and (2) understand what our relationship with God can be.

In infancy, children quickly learn that "everyone has been put on earth to meet *my* needs." A few years later, adolescents may generalize: "God's job is to take care of *my* needs. After all, I'm his child." Most of us spend the remainder of our lives unlearning this. Marriage helps us learn that we must meet *others'* needs. We soon learn through marriage that our beloved's agenda may not be simply to follow behind us and meet all our needs. Often the sounds of family living are the screech and whine of gears seeking to mesh and knocking rough spots off each other as they grind away at their tasks.

By experiencing intimacy with a spouse, we learn the feelings and obligations of intimacy. Once we have recognized that our spouse has a unique personality and individual needs and is not content to be a mere extension of our will, we sometimes can transfer that learning and realize that God, too, is a personality, not merely an extension of our will. This learning can revolutionize our prayer life, helping us pray more fluently in adoration, thanksgiving, praise and confession.

Marriage is one of God's principal means of teaching humans about his triune nature. Marriage teaches us that we cannot control every part of life, and that drives us to seek God's fatherly care.

God also reveals himself as Jesus through marriage. As we find the need for sacrificial love, for laying down our will at the feet of our beloved, we understand some of the magnitude of what Jesus did for us. We also learn forgiveness. We all sin against our beloved at times; a marriage survives only through confession of our faults and sins to our beloved, and it thrives only in forgiveness when we have been wronged. It is through Jesus that we are forgiven, and if we heed the lessons from marriage, we are freed to practice confession and receive forgiveness from God.

Finally, God uses marriage to reveal himself as the Holy Spirit. The Spirit is confronter, comforter and counselor, and we find each of these roles to be central to healthy marriage. At times, I need confrontation about my behavior. In Kirby, my spouse, I find a lover who reluctantly risks my anger and rejection because she knows I need to face the darkness within my soul. Lovingly and sensitively, she is able to help me see my conscious or unconscious sins and mistakes. When I sense her abiding comfort, I also learn about the faithfulness and care of the Holy Spirit.

Becoming One Flesh

Marriage forges a couple into a unified, yet differentiated whole, which the Bible calls "one flesh." The union is spiritual in that it ties together the partners' spirits under the watchfulness of God. The union is physical in that husband and wife join their bodies in the intimate act of sexual intercourse, which the Bible often refers to as "knowing" each other. The union is psychological in that the personality of each spouse is shaped in response to the other. The union is also social, for people treat the couple as a couple rather than as two individuals, and the couple defines itself as a dyad. Thus, partners' entire beings are united.

The physical body is living and continually changing, yet despite its constant transformability, it is remarkably stable. Similarly, a marriage is also transformed continually by intimate interaction between lovers, yet, in spite of the changes, marriages tend to be remarkably similar from year to year.

Bodies of flesh pass through different ages during which different life tasks are addressed. Marriage has similar ages requiring different tasks. In its infancy, marriage tests the self-centeredness of both partners and requires that they learn to share. In its adolescence, the partners remain in union but work to establish their own lives with their own particular missions. In its early adulthood, marriage incorporates children, and the vestiges of self-centeredness can be dealt with as parents rear a family. In its middle years, the marriage overcomes routine and remains vital in love and child rearing. In the marriage's later years, the partners reestablish themselves as a dyad and come to terms with the meaning of their relationship.

Marital commitment ebbs and flows throughout the marriage. Divorces peak in the third, seventh, and seventeenth through twentieth years of marriage. Marital contentment also changes over the course of a marriage.

Usually, satisfied couples report their highest contentment with marriage in the early years, after they have weathered an adjustment period that comes about halfway through the first year of marriage. With the birth of their first child, the typical satisfied couple becomes less contented with the marriage. When the first child enters school, contentment again suffers. When the first child enters adolescence, marital contentment of wives is low, but husbands' contentment is at its very lowest ebb.

During the "launching period," when the adolescent children are leaving home, husbands begin to feel more contented with the marriage, but wives often come into their lowest period of marital satisfaction. Once the children are away, though, tne marital contentment of both husbands and wives rebounds to a high level.[1]

The relative contentment of troubled couples follows a similar trajectory during the early years of marriage—one of steady decline with each passing stage. These couples' marital contentment is substantially below that of satisfied couples. And once children leave home, troubled couples often suffer less and less contentment in their marriages.[2]

The one flesh of marriage is imperfect. When we marry, we acknowledge that our spouse is not perfect, but we usually can't see the imperfections clearly. As time ticks by, though, we may get peeved, bothered, even downright angry at certain things our spouse does. The emotional disappointments eventually crowd out our early biases and give us a different picture of our spouse. Sometimes the picture is more realistic, incorporating strengths and weaknesses. At other times, though, the disappointments, anger and bitterness of violated expectations can bias us against our spouse, preventing us from seeing the excellent attributes we had so easily seen when we were first married.

Flesh sometimes is bruised, cut, hurt or broken. At those times, God heals us. Doctors, counselors and our own efforts may speed healing and keep us from interfering with God's healing, but God deserves the glory for sustaining marriage and healing it when necessary.

A Flexible Ideal

All marriages are different, because all individuals are unique and the ways their personalities meld during marriage itself is unique. Not only are all marriages in fact different, but the ideal marriage—the vision— is also different for each couple.

Individuals are unique. We all have the same fundamental need—for meaning. We all try to achieve that need through intimacy and action. Yet we differ in the ways we show intimacy and affect each other.

Relationships differ too. Despite the adage that opposites attract, research has consistently shown that similarities are most important in our selection of friends and mates.[3] Yet, even when spouses are similar to each other, their relationship has its own unique characteristics.

Nicholas, thirty-year-old muscle-weary basketball player, and Brenda, soon-to-be new mother, have a warm intimacy in which they can both banter and talk deeply. Yet they still differ over sexual intimacy. Nicholas enjoys physical affection and likes to caress Brenda sexually throughout the day. Brenda doesn't like his caresses except when they are making love, which they do two or three times each week. In bed, they are traditional in their lovemaking. Although they have an excellent sexual relationship, Brenda and Nicholas sometimes struggle over their daytime sexual behavior.

Danielle and Gus, married for thirty-two years, also have an excellent marriage, yet their sexual relationship doesn't resemble Nicholas and Brenda's. During their marriage Danielle and Gus have had many separations that gave them little opportunity for sexual relationship. First there was the army; then Gus had a job that required him to travel extensively. Finally, Danielle began a program at a university that was about one hundred miles away, so that she had to be away from home four days a week. This couple's pattern of sexual intimacy involved what they called "sex binges." They made love three or four times during a weekend—but usually they could make love only about one weekend per month. Their lovemaking was more uninhibited than Nicholas and Brenda's.

Both couples are satisfied with their sexual relationship, but the relationships are different. The two couples have different needs, and each partner has different needs, yet the partners communicate and work out sexual practices that satisfy each person.

Whether in sexual relationship or other aspects of the marriage, the scriptural ideal for marriage is not a rigid set of guidelines. The scriptural ideal is that *partners try to please each other and govern their behavior by scriptural principles, with each couple creating a unique vision of what God intends for their marriage.*

God makes sure that our needs are met. God meets many of our needs by giving us a lifelong marital partner. It's important to remember, though, that not all of our needs—except sexual needs—can be met by a spouse. God also provides church friends, family members and daily activities to help meet our needs.

The Structure of a Marriage

Each marriage grows from the partners' vision of what their marriage can be. The vision of mutual love is like the frame that holds a building together. Without the frame, the building would crumble under stress. And without a vision of marriage, the building blocks of marriage cannot hold together.

Commitment and contentment are two large building blocks of marriage. Imagine that only two levels of contentment are possible, high and low; picture the same for commitment. We might expect that high contentment and high commitment would always go together, but actually that's not so. The four possible combinations are shown as four boxes in figure 1.

In the top box are couples who are high in both contentment and commitment. We'll call these people the *Consummate Couple*. The second box, high commitment and low contentment, is a category for

CONTENTMENT

		High	Low
COMMITMENT	**High**	*consummate couple*	*faithful feuders dulled darlings*
	Low	*alcoholic workaholic momaholic*	*divorce prone*

Figure 1. Types of marriages showing relationships between marital contentment and marital commitment.

people who have been married for years and are not contented with their marriage. They may be *Faithful Feuders,* who remain together despite chronic conflict, or they may be *Dulled Darlings,* who have lost all intimacy but can't give up the companionship of the spouse. It is also easy to think of couples in the third box, those contented with their relationship yet not committed to it. Usually, those *Loose Lovers* have sexual affairs or betray the relationship in other ways such as being alcoholic, workaholic, or even "momaholic" (so committed to the children that the marriage is in trouble). Finally, some couples are low in both commitment and contentment. These couples, *Soon-to-Be Sad Statistics,* are usually headed for divorce unless something changes.

The reason that contentment and commitment don't always march in tandem is that commitment is related not only to contentment but also to *investments* within the relationship and to *competitors* to the marriage. I will explain this idea in chapter eleven.

The foundation of contentment is confession and forgiveness within the marriage. A positive vision for marriage must contain provision for confession and forgiveness, because humans are imperfect. Occasions for confession and forgiveness are found in closeness, communication, conflict resolution and causal inference (attributing responsibility or blame). Each of those areas is like a room built on the foundation of confession and forgiveness.

Based on how couples handle those aspects of their marriage, they will be more or less contented. Their contentment depends on whether their closeness, communication, conflict resolution and causal inferences are perceived to be rewarding or costly. Contentment also depends on the ways that the rewards or costs differ from the partners' expectations.

The remainder of this book helps you assess your marriage in each main area of marriage: confession and forgiveness, closeness, communication, conflict resolution, causal attributions, commitment. Then, based on your systematic assessment, you can change your marriage relationship in the areas that need the most attention.

2

The Blurred Vision: What Causes Marital Problems?

I shifted uncomfortably in my chair and looked at the reporter. "What *causes* marital problems?" I repeated. "Is this a trick question?"

She smiled, trying to put me at ease. "No, our readers really would like to know what causes most marital problems. Is it mothers-in-law, financial problems, religious differences or what?"

Suddenly, I had the answer. I smiled triumphantly and said, "Yes."

"Yes," she repeated, dumbfounded. "Yes, what? This is not helpful, Mr. Worthington."

I noted that I'd been demoted from "Dr. Worthington," which was how she had begun the interview. "Yes, *all* of those cause marital problems," I said.

"No, I mean, what causes problems in a single marriage? I know that each of those causes problems in different marriages. But what is the most frequent cause of marital problems?

I took a deep breath, knowing my answer would probably earn me another demotion, perhaps to "Everett' or "you slippery weasel." "My niece has strep throat, which is caused by bacteria," I finally said. "My son has a sore foot, which was caused by twisting his ankle. But marital problems aren't caused by a germ or a single event. They have many causes at the same time."

"Oh," the reporter said. She probably thought, *Oh, brother.* She was no longer taking notes.

"The 'cause' depends on what purpose I intend to use the cause for."

"That sounds very subjective and unscientific," she said. She scribbled something down on her note pad. My fantasies of what she was writing did not encourage me.

"Let's take an analogy," I said. "Suppose a man sat on a hill and pressed the button on a flashlight in a da-da-da, de-de-de, da-da-da pattern. The cause of his actions could be explained in several ways. A physicist would explain the light in terms of electrochemical reactions within the battery and transmission of light waves of a given frequency and amplitude through space. A neurologist would explain the behavior in terms of the electrical impulses flowing down neuronal pathways. An anatomist would say the cause was muscular contractions. A spy would immediately recognize that the man's behavior was caused by his need for help, which prompted the SOS signal."

"So you're saying that the understanding of the cause of marital problems depends on who's explaining the cause," she said.

"*And* for what purpose," I added.

"For instance?" She raised her left eyebrow.

"For instance, if a wife were explaining why marital problems were occurring, she might talk about her husband's provocative behavior."

"I see," she said. "And the husband wouldn't agree. And you're saying, Ev, that neither would be incorrect."

I heard the "Ev" go by and knew that either we were getting chummier or I was going to look like Jerk-of-the-Year in the Sunday supplement. "I'd rather say that if both spouses continue to view the cause of their difficulties from their own point of view, they will continue to have marital problems. But if they want a different outcome, such as improving their marriage, they need to understand the causes differently."

"Well, Mr. Worthington, what would you recommend?"

"Accepting their own responsibility in causing the marital difficulties would be helpful for each spouse, but they could actually improve more by looking for specific causes of difficulties that they can modify."

"Okay, doc, tell me about those specific causes."

Professor Says Causes of Marriage Problems Are Many

Unmet expectations, difficult life situations, individual problems, and relationship characteristics are major causes of marital problems, according to VCU professor and licensed Clinical Psychologist Everett Worthington. "The difficulty," said Worthington, "is that all of the causes can be acting at the same time."

About one hundred years ago, William James, one of the first psychologists, targeted unmet expectations as the cause of unhappiness. Engaged couples always marry their romantic ideal of the spouse rather than the spouse. When the wedding gifts are boxed up and the new wears off, the partners confront the real partner, complete with warts, and not the romantic ideal. The shock devastates many marriages.

Cindy Lou and Vernon Peters have been married seven months. They confess to being somewhat disillusioned with each other but maintain that they still are deeply in love. "The first disillusionment," said Cindy Lou, "was in our third month of marriage. We had a chance to go country and western dancing, and Vernon refused to go. He said that he had gone dancing before we were married just because he wanted to be with me, but he really hated dancing. I was crushed. The man I married wasn't the man I married."

Vernon told of his own disappointment. "Cindy Lou and I had always gone to all kinds of activities together. After we were married, it seemed she just wanted to sit around and read. I didn't understand that at all. I didn't even know she liked to read."

Cindy Lou and Vernon have worked through their adjustments, but both describe months of emotional turmoil before they settled down.

Difficult life situations also cause marital problems. Family scientists Charles Figley and Hamilton McCubbin have identified a host of stressful family events such as unemployment, rape, death of a child, disaster, abandonment, and war, that can intensify marital tensions. If the catastrophic event is of sufficient magnitude, Figley says that "the event will disrupt the lifestyle and routine of the survivors, cause a sense of destruction, disruption and loss, [and create] a permanent and detailed memory of the event which may be recalled voluntarily or involuntarily."[1]

Harvey Myers had worked as a vice-president in a large company for ten years when he was fired because the product he managed was discontinued. Harvey was unable to get a job for over a year. "During that time, I almost drove my wife Katherine crazy," he said. "I came into her domain uninvited and applied my managerial skills to streamlining the household operation. When Katherine had to take a job to support us, I felt I was no longer a man. I became depressed and got addicted to soap operas. It was a bad year." After a time, Harvey was hired as a night watchman, which restored some of his self-esteem. Only with marriage counseling did Harvey and Katherine restore their relationship. Katherine said, "We had marital tension even before Harvey lost his job. The job was the straw that broke the camel's back."

"Individual problems can add strains to an even well-functioning marriage," said Worthington. "One married client had unipolar manic episodes. At times, for no external reason, he would have high energy, overconfidence, little sleep, extreme talkativeness, and a tendency to make bad decisions—all part of his psychological disorder." Worthington described the effects of impaired decision making on the marriage. During one manic episode, the man sold his house, bought a plantation, and borrowed over one million dollars to purchase a new business. Although his wife was committed to the marriage, living with the uncertainties of the illness made her uneasy about their future. During the times that were not in his manic cycle, the couple arranged their affairs so that damage done during a manic episode would be limited. Nonetheless, living under the threat of future manic episodes, even with medication that kept the mania largely under control, created constant marital stress.

Relationship characteristics are another source of marital stress. Patricia Noller, a social scientist who has investigated marital communication for years, has repeatedly found that spouses who can communicate well with strangers often communicate poorly with their own partners.[2] Poor communication is often not an individual problem. It is a relationship problem. Worthington explained, "A marriage is a relationship with a long history. Usually, over time spouses have tried to communicate in a variety of ways. Some couples become frustrated with the results. They burn out on 'healthy' communication strategies with their partner and over the years become more coercive. Even though the partners continue to communicate well with strangers and friends, they can't seem to be civil with each other."

Worthington blames the power struggle for most unhealthy conflict. Power struggles are simply disagreements over who has the power to make decisions. These should not be confused with the topic under discussion. One couple disagreed chronically over their vacation plans. The husband wanted to go to the beach and the wife wanted to vacation in the mountains. One day, the husband proposed a compromise—the lake. The wife refused. She suggested getting a cabin at a nearby state park. "The couple were not really arguing over where to vacation. They were involved in a power struggle over *who could say* where they were to vacation," said Worthington.

A couple that wants a happy marriage should be more concerned with solving their problems than with merely naming them, according to Worthington. Solving problems means that the problems must be identified in a way that will allow the couple to do something about the problems, something more than blame the spouse for the problem. Spouses are advised to identify their own unrealistic expectations, remain supportive during and after crises, plan ways to deal constructively with individual problems before the problems are at a crisis level, and avoid power struggles and unfruitful blaming and coercive problem solving strategies. If the couple practices these guidelines, many marital struggles can be avoided or solved.

I tossed aside the newspaper and speculated about the article. I was pleased that the reporter had captured the essence of our conversation, but the brevity of the article meant that many important aspects of marital problems had not been covered. Each of the four types of problems was illustrated by only a single case, while there are many examples of unmet expectations, difficult situations, individual problems and relationship characteristics that contribute to marital stress. Let's take our time as we examine these issues here.

Unmet Expectations

Psychologist Arnold Lazarus, in *Marital Myths,* and psychiatrist Aaron Beck, in *Love Is Never Enough,* identify a variety of marital myths that lead to troubled relationships.[3] Beck proposes nine steps that can help couples change such mental distortions.

☐ Link negative emotional reactions with automatic thoughts that are causing the reactions.

☐ Use imagination to identify negative thoughts rather than wait for troubling situations to occur.

☐ Practice identifying automatic thoughts such as "he's hopeless," "she's completely self-centered," or "he never does anything right." Automatic thoughts are not easy to recognize unless you practice.

☐ Use replay techniques to recall past situations that have been upsetting and to identify negative thinking in those situations.

☐ Question automatic thoughts. Examine evidence on which automatic thoughts are based, and ask how sure you are that you know your spouse's motives.

☐ Use rational responses rather than jumping irrationally to conclusions.

☐ Test your predictions. For example, you might expect that expressing a never-before-stated wish to stay home for Christmas rather than travel to see the in-laws will provoke an argument. You could test the prediction by carefully planning a nonhurtful way to discuss the topic.

☐ Reframe negative thoughts by considering negative qualities in another light. For example, nagging might be understood as care and concern.

☐ Label your distortions by recognizing and talking with your spouse about how you typically allow negative expectations to intrude in your marriage. Rather than trying to help your spouse eliminate his or her negative expectations, concentrate on your own.

Of course, listing these guidelines is easier than applying them. When our expectations are violated, we naturally feel hurt and angry, become emotional and think about how much we have been wronged. Yet solving marital problems usually requires just the opposite of the natural response: self-discipline, unselfishness and a greater desire to resolve differences than to win marital struggles.

Difficult Situations

A close friend and I sat in a restaurant comparing athletic injuries and lamenting the ravages of age. The friend began telling me about his father-in-law, who had recently been diagnosed with Alzheimer's disease. The disease was in the early stages, causing general apathy and a few lapses in memory.

With tears in his eyes, my friend described the progression of Alzheimer's disease. Early memory disturbances become more profound until affected people forget how to drive, what their address is or where the bathroom is in their own house. In the final stage, the person may fail to recognize anyone—even his or her spouse; the victim may undergo personality changes, become violent or verbally abusive, eventually lapse into a coma and die. The degeneration can be relatively rapid or agonizingly slow, eating up a couple's life savings for hospital or nursing care. "I know that suicide is wrong," said my friend, "but I don't know what I'd do if I thought that my disease would destroy my family financially and perhaps psychologically as well. I just don't know."

There are no easy answers to my friend's worries. Alzheimer's takes a dreadful toll not only on the person with the disease but also on the spouse, who faces years of sacrifice and care for one who may become unappreciative, even abusive. The victim's change in personality can make the sacrifice seem as if it were being made for a stranger. Marriage commitment is severely taxed.

Alzheimer's is only one difficult situation that can confront the marriage. Others might be a chronically ill child, job-mandated separations, a disabling accident, a natural disaster. Each creates unique stresses on the marriage, making the relationship seem more costly and less rewarding.

Individual Problems
A mental disorder such as depression, schizophrenia, or character disorder forces individuals to deal with their psychological pain, places a burden of care—including financial and emotional support—on spouses and other family members, and requires the individual's family to deal with social stigma and misunderstanding. Marriages often unravel with the strain. The affected spouse may not be able to cope with the problem or to handle the guilt of the burdens he or she is inflicting on

the spouse. The partner may feel that caring for the spouse is more than was bargained for within the marriage agreement. He or she may walk out.

Alcoholism and drug abuse also affect marriage. Often the drug-dependent spouse has a limited tolerance for intimacy and uses alcohol or drugs to manage intimacy. In other instances, the alcoholic or drug abuser uses a substance to loosen inhibitions so that anger, sadness, or even affection can be expressed. Some people use substances to gain new experiences of feeling high, while others use drugs to numb their feelings or forget their pain. Regardless of the reason for the abuse, a couple's interactions when one partner is "under the influence" are often destructive to the relationship.

Less severe personal disturbances can also wreck marriages. Uncontrolled anger, compulsive spending or gambling, irresponsibility in getting or holding jobs, selfishness, unforgiveness and a critical spirit can poison the marriage relationship.

Relationship Problems

Most marital problems don't affect just one spouse; they involve relationship difficulties. The relationship is more than the sum of the individuals' contributions. Relationship difficulties occur because of the partners' history with each other.

The root cause of systemic marital discord is sin and selfishness. Sin and selfishness elevate each partner's needs and wants for *closeness or distance* above those of the spouse. Sin and selfishness create me-centered *communication,* in which the partners do not think of each other's needs; each attempts to manipulate the partner to meet his or her own needs. Sin and selfishness frustrate *conflict resolution* because they establish a win-lose mentality that results in a power struggle; well-practiced conflict-negotiation strategies maintain the power struggle. Sin and selfishness whisper *accusations* against the partner and prime the ear to listen to and believe the accusations. At the center of all of these relationship difficulties is an attitude of self-righteous self-justification that proclaims, "I'm right. My partner's wrong. My partner's to blame." Finally, sin and selfishness erode *commitment.*

The Rumpelstiltskin Myth

Marriages involve the complicated intertwining of two lives under God's care and guidance. This threefold cord is not easily broken (see Eccl 4:12), yet it does tend to unravel if not cared for. Part of caring for the marriage is to understand some of the causes of marital distress and find ways to change the marriage when it needs repair and healing.

Reading the Sunday-supplement article on marital problems, I was dissatisfied because it omitted many potential causes of marital difficulties, but the biggest problem with the article was that it encapsulated what I called the Rumpelstiltskin myth.

In the fairy tale "Rumpelstiltskin," a miller makes a deal with the king that if the miller's daughter can spin straw into gold, then the king will allow the prince to marry the miller's daughter. Both the miller and the king are lured by the promise of instant wealth. Alas, the miller's daughter cannot perform. On three successive nights, a magical dwarf, Rumpelstiltskin, takes the poor girl's only possessions and finally extracts a promise of the soon-to-be princess's firstborn child as his fees for spinning her straw into gold. All are happy—until the child is born.

On the first night home from the hospital, the princess sits holding her new baby and, no doubt, contemplating the limitations of her Lamaze childbirth classes. Poof! The dwarf appears and demands the child, finally agreeing to give up his claim on the child only if the princess can guess his name within three days.

On the last day, the princess discovers the secret, and that night, she triumphantly announces the dwarf's name: Rumpelstiltskin! The dwarf is (understandably) miffed, and showing poor impulse control, he stamps his foot so hard that he rips himself apart, solving the princess's problems forever.

Repeatedly throughout the story we find the search for an easy solution to one's difficulties. Even the climax of the story embodies the point: simply name your problem and it will disappear. This is the Rumpelstiltskin myth.

The Rumpelstiltskin myth is appealing because knowing how to label our problems gives us a sense of control over them. That is helpful because a sense of control often encourages us to tackle painful problems. Yet marital difficulties will not simply disintegrate once they have been named, as the article implied. Couples must deal with marital difficulties through prayer, changed attitudes and focused action. In the following chapter, we discuss how you can begin to change your marriage.

3

A Vision
of Healing

About five years ago, I hurt my foot while jogging. Since I had long been involved in competitive tennis and soccer, normal aches and pains of exertion were common; in fact, the ice bag and heating pad were two of my best friends. I immediately ministered to my sore foot by soaking it in an ice bath.

For the next two weeks, my foot remained sore and swollen. Eventually, out of frustration, I went to the orthopedist. "What seems to be the problem?" he asked.

"I have a sore toe. It's not really too bad. I have taken a lot of aspirin, and I soak it about four times a day in ice water."

"How effective is that?"

"It feels better after I soak it. It doesn't bother me much except when I put pressure on the toe."

The orthopedist diagnosed my problem as "jogger's toe," an inflamed tendon in the foot. He gave me some anti-inflammatory medication. Unfortunately, I was allergic to the medicine. On Thanksgiving, I developed seven mouth ulcers and watched everyone else enjoy a delicious turkey dinner with all the fixings.

I went to another orthopedist. He, too, diagnosed my malady as jogger's toe. I was skeptical. Bad decision on my part. He pushed the toe down hard. That catapulted my rigid body straight into the air, where I initiated breathing patterns I had learned in Lamaze childbirth classes. This orthopedist taught me a valuable lesson—never question his judgment.

Two weeks later, the foot again ballooned. I went back to orthopedist number one, who had the foot x-rayed using the left-footed reverse convoluted half-angled projection, or some other fancy technique. This required me to assume a position on the x-ray table that a rubber man at the circus would have found difficult. There was—you guessed it— a break where the ligaments from two toes connected to the ball of the foot. Every time I put any weight on it, the break was pulled apart. It took forever to heal.

Broken Bones, Broken Marriages

While my foot healed, I carried on with my counseling, research, writing and teaching about marriage. As I watched troubled marriages being healed and at the same time experienced the healing of my troubled foot, I began to appreciate many similarities.

I noticed how breaks in bones and marriages are often not apparent during the early stages. Only a few breaks are compound fractures, which are apparent to everyone when the broken bones thrust their jagged edges through the skin. In those cases, the danger of infection adds additional risk to the injury.

But most of the time, people in a fractured marriage do as I did— try home remedies that might have worked in the past, put off going to the doctor, and gimp along using an irregular gait and favoring the tender parts. Yet, beneath the skin, the bone continues to ache. Like my ice-and-aspirin treatment of my broken foot, sometimes people soothe the aches or broken love with alcohol or drugs, by throwing themselves into work or by flirting with others.

Good diagnosis is essential to good treatment. I couldn't make a proper diagnosis of my foot problem because I had never broken a bone before. Even the doctor was fooled, because I had minimized the symptoms and didn't show much pain. I didn't *want* my foot to be broken. Not only did I not have previous experience with broken bones, but I didn't even know the symptoms of a broken bone.

Similarly, when people begin to feel marital stress, it often scares them. They don't *want* to become a divorce statistic, so they refuse to acknowledge that there may be fractures in their relationship. They may not even know what to look for and thus how to deal with the difficulties.

In this book, I try to help you diagnose your marriage problems. However, if the book doesn't answer your most crucial questions, it may be appropriate to seek the opinion of a pastor or counselor who can give you specific feedback about your marriage.

For my bone to heal, the two severed pieces needed to remain in contact. When I walked on the foot, the weight continually pulled apart the bones, preventing healing.

In a marriage, the two parts of the one flesh must also remain together if healing is to occur. This does not mean that separation is not sometimes necessary. It is often helpful in cases of physical abuse or to break up patterns of extremely destructive arguing. For marriages to be healed, troublesome patterns of low intimacy, lack of caring, poor communication, high conflict or blame must be suspended, or at least drastically reduced. Love must be given a chance to grow again.

Bones heal from the outside in. A soft tissue bridge forms across the broken pieces. Over time, the bridge hardens, which permits the bone tissues to knit together underneath the protective bridge.

In marriages that require repair, we must also change some of the external forms. Only when those forms are changed will the inner marriage—the joining of spirit, soul and body—recombine into a whole flesh.

Thus, to allow my bone to heal, I had to do some "unnatural" acts. I had to wear a cast for months. I had to hobble on crutches, even after I was promoted from heavy plaster to a removable plastic cast. There is nothing natural about wearing a cast or pole-vaulting around on crutches. But the unnaturalness of the treatment helped the bone to knit together.

To help a fractured marriage heal, it is often necessary to do "unnatural" things. Couples who attend marriage counseling are often instructed to caress each other's bodies without the expectation of sexual intercourse to help restore sexual intimacy, communicate in seemingly rigid patterns to ensure that each person hears and understands the other, resolve differences through a method that is foreign to them, and stop noticing what the spouse is doing *wrong* and begin noticing what he or she is doing to promote a healthier marriage.

I chafed restlessly as my foot healed. *This broken foot is cutting into my tennis playing,* I thought. I strained to rush back to the tennis court. *Be patient. Give the healing time.* In my mind, I knew that healing took time, but having patience to wait was a different story. I knew that God would eventually heal my foot if I didn't exert my will to prevent the healing. But the will is strong, and it often demands that the mind obey it rather than meekly submitting to the mind. Waiting was a continual struggle, especially as the foot began to feel better. When the foot was sore, I hadn't been as tempted to return to my old ways as when the foot was nearly well and the frustration of tennis deprivation had built up.

Patience is also required as God heals a fractured marriage. Spouses long to put behind them the communication patterns that have not yet become second nature. They acknowledge God's work in their relationship, unconsciously hoping that recognizing his work will make it come to fruition faster and will relieve them of the burden of practicing new behavior until it has become automatic. The temptation is greater as couples improve their communication and reestablish closeness, trust and forgiveness. The mind knows that complete healing takes time, but the will shouts loudly, trying to drown out the reasoned advice of the mind. So the couple must heed only the mind, allowing God to heal fully.

The Complications of Healing
Once I knew that my broken foot had healed, I tested my weight on

it tentatively. I did not rip the cast off and rush out to a hopscotch tournament on the same day.

Likewise, when a marriage has been healing, partners shouldn't rush to test the relationship by provoking the spouse.

Once the bone is healed, it may be even stronger at the fracture point than it was before the break. An extra thickness of bone tissue may reinforce the area. However, the extra thickness of bone tissue may bring other complications, such as favoring the tender foot until other muscles are strained, or developing a bone spur that keeps the tissue around the fracture tender even though the fracture itself is healed.

In this regard, too, a healing marriage is not unlike a healing bone. Although fractured communication may have been repaired, the couple may have adjusted their lifestyle to avoid conflict, and those adjustments continue even after the couple has gained the communication tools to deal with conflict. Or new areas of discord may arise even as a consequence of the healing.

One couple I counseled some years ago seemed to delight in putting each other down. Painstakingly, we identified the ways they devalued each other, and the couple worked hard to build up rather than put down. They finished counseling much in love, having learned to avoid put-downs.

But about a year and a half later, they contacted me for additional counseling. Over time, they had developed a new pattern of putting each other down: they seemed to delight in noticing each other's use of put-down strategies that we had identified during the earlier counseling. It was as if the healing bridge forged in marital therapy had become the source of later irritation. Only when each spouse could focus on his or her own put-downs rather than on the other's did their marriage stop being troublesome.

For many people, healing a broken bone is not the end of their difficulties. They are plagued by atrophied muscles after the broken bone has mended. The body silently cries for corrective exercises that stretch and strengthen muscles, then protests when we heed its demands. Yet we must get the muscles back in balance after the broken bone has forced new muscles to take additional strain and other muscles to wither from disuse. New body positions and postures have left us off-balance, with vague aches and pains.

Self-discipline is tested as we ignore the protests of our weakened muscles and tell them to work as they should. Some of us may give in and take the easy road, telling ourselves that time will put our body back into balance. Indeed, it usually will—if we don't hurt ourselves in the meantime. But using vigilance and self-control to force ourselves to exercise will reap dividends of more rapid return to normality and balance.

Some people have difficulty making themselves exercise or may not know exactly how to put the body's musculature back into balance. They may need to employ a physical therapist to assist them. The physical therapist is an external director who can instruct and help motivate the flagging will. Yet despite the technical assistance and gadgetry of the physical therapist, the patient must still complete the exercises if he or she is to benefit.

In the same way, many people can repair a damaged marriage by themselves, suffering the discomfort and unease of reestablishing new patterns of behavior. But others are either not knowledgeable or not self-disciplined enough to take that route. They need the assistance of the external expert—the pastor or the counselor.

It is not more (or less) noble to solve one's physical or marital difficulties without help. The true question we must ask is, What method will yield the best return? In pursuing physical health or marital health, the person who is wise will use the resources available to help reach the goal.

The goal, though, is all-important. In the following chapter, we focus more specifically on your goals for your marriage.

4

Bringing
the Vision
into Focus

What specifically do you want to be different in your life as a result of reading this book? Please *write* the answer to this question, giving as much detail as you can.

If you are like most people, you will not have written the answer by the time you read this sentence. That's okay. You might not need to write the answer. It might help, though, to write the answer, and I urge you to take pen in hand and use it throughout the remainder of the book. I suggest that you write, "My goal is to make my marriage better than it is right now."

Now, carefully consider your marriage. Which of the following statements comes the closest to describing your marriage? Circle the number or write it on a separate piece of paper.

1. Perfect. Couldn't be better.

2. Wonderful. Any marriage could be improved, but I don't see exactly how my marriage could improve at this time.

3. Excellent. I know of a few specific improvements I would like to see, but I'm very satisfied with my marriage.

4. Very Good. We have a few times when we are not close, a few glitches in communication, a few recurring conflicts and a few times we hurt each other, but overall I am quite satisfied with my marriage.

5. Good. We have some periodic problems in closeness, communication, conflict and confession/forgiveness, and occasionally we have some quite hurtful interactions. I am satisfied with my marriage more than half of the time.

6. Fair. We have more hurtful interactions and more problems than I think we should, but we still love and enjoy each other. I think we should do something to help our relationship or it could grow worse.

7. In Some Trouble. We have substantial problems that have worsened in the last six months. I am getting worried about the future of our relationship. If something doesn't change, we are probably in trouble.

8. Definitely in Trouble. We have substantial problems that have lasted longer than six months. I am worried about the future of my marriage—about my happiness, about the possibility of divorce or separation, or both. I think we must do something to change the relationship soon, or we will be in deep trouble.

9. Little Hope. We have severe problems in closeness, communication, conflict and confession/forgiveness. Either we have separated or at least one of us has contacted a lawyer.

Your use of this book depends on how you assess the health of your marriage.

☐ If you circled 1 (Perfect) or 2 (Wonderful), then you are probably seeking the inspiration from this book to act constructively to make a good marriage better.

☐ If you circled 3 (Excellent), you are probably *also* seeking education about some specific things you could do to improve your marriage.

☐ If you circled 4 (Very Good) or 5 (Good), then besides inspiration and education you are probably also seeking the time and willingness to act differently when stress and problems occur.

☐ If you circled 6 (Fair), you probably want inspiration, education, help at stress points and the willingness to forgive hurts and to act in a concerted way to heal difficulties.

☐ If you circled 7 (In Some Trouble) or 8 (Definitely in Trouble), you may be looking for all of the above plus a willingness to change and to persevere even when you fail.

☐ If you circled 9 (Little Hope), you may seek a resurgence of hope and the resolve not to hurt each other, children, family or friends as you try to reconcile your relationship.

☐ Generally, if you circled 7, 8 or 9, you should at least consider seeking marital counseling.

At the beginning of this section, I suggested that you write your answer to a question. If your primary goal in reading this book is inspiration or education, then reading alone will likely provide those. But your marriage probably won't change a lot through reading alone. Change usually requires concrete action and attention to specifics. So if you rated your marriage at 4 through 9, you should write your answers to questions I pose throughout the book. To make this easier, questions and suggestions requiring action are highlighted with open boxes.

In general, self-help books suffer from a common weakness, regardless of how skillfully written they are. They are written for people with a variety of problems rather than being targeted at the specific problems of individuals. I want *you* to be able to benefit from this book, but you must know your specific objectives to know how you can benefit.

Your Goals for Your Marriage

Let's identify some of your goals. Answer each of the following questions.

☐ 1. If you woke up the day after completing this book and your marriage was much better than it is now, exactly what would be different?

☐ 2. How would you know that the marriage had improved? For example, would your feelings be different? Would your spouse's actions be different? Would yours?

☐ 3. How would your spouse know that the marriage had improved? Suppose you couldn't tell him or her about the differences. What would your spouse observe to be different?

☐ 4. Would change have been sudden, gradual or herky-jerky? Would there have been intermediate steps? Plateaus?

Answering these questions will help you reflect on how you would like *your* marriage to be. It will help you begin to form a positive vision of *your* marriage and its possibilities.

Do We Need Professional Counseling?

By now you have a general picture of your marriage satisfaction and an idea of how you would like your marriage to be better. If your marriage is troubled, you may be wondering whether you should try to work on the problems by yourselves or whether to contact a marital therapist or a pastor who regularly does marital therapy.

In table 1, I have listed some indications that should lead you to consider seeing a professional. Probably the best general guideline is to seek professional help when individual or marital problems are severe and resistant to change. Although many problems could be easily remedied if couples sought help *before* they became severe, if you're like most people, you'll try to solve moderate problems yourself, or with the help of friends and family, and you'll seek professional help only for tough, persistent problems.

What Happens in Marital Counseling?

If you attend counseling, your experiences will depend on the counselor's approach. Usually, counselors prefer to see both partners rather than only one, and your chances of improving your marriage are greatly improved if both of you attend counseling.[1]

Most marital therapists like to meet with partners weekly, for six to twenty sessions over a period of two months to a half a year. Regular meetings help a couple focus on changing their relationship because they must report their efforts to the counselor. Not all therapists agree, but I have found that couples can count on a minimum of six sessions. More sessions may be needed if marital problems have been long-lasting or very serious.

Table 1. Some indications that you may want to seek marital counseling.

- ☐ Someone is getting physically hurt or suffering such damage to self-esteem that he or she is seriously depressed or troubled.

- ☐ Alcohol or drug dependency is involved.

- ☐ Marital problems have existed for a long time and seem to be getting worse.

- ☐ Marital problems have existed for a long time. You have tried almost everything you know to aid the marriage, and nothing has worked.

- ☐ Sexual difficulties such as premature ejaculation, impotence, failure to have orgasms, or painful intercourse have become a serious strain.

- ☐ One or both partners have serious emotional or personal difficulties that seem to be caused by or causing marital difficulties.

- ☐ Children are frequently getting caught in the midst of marital arguments.

- ☐ Either person is distressed enough to think marriage counseling is necessary.

- ☐ Either person has contacted a lawyer.

- ☐ Either person is having or has recently had an affair.

- ☐ You appear locked into a power struggle, or you have several differences that you've been unable to resolve through persistent effort.

- ☐ Either spouse feels unable to forgive the partner for some past transgression.

- ☐ Either spouse is allowing outside activities to reduce family time to near zero, and this absence of commitment seriously distresses the other spouse.

- ☐ Personal or marital tensions are increasing rapidly.

- ☐ Either spouse is trying to force the partner to act or be a way not agreed upon by the partner.

Marital therapists try to keep arguments from getting out of hand. Therapists may have the couple discuss their differences, but they generally try to keep the couple from arguing destructively. Couples usually think the counselor wants to help them resolve their differences, but most counselors are more interested in helping the couple learn *how* to resolve *any* differences they have than in helping them arrive at specific solutions to a few current problems.

All therapists try to help couples communicate better, but therapists' methods vary. There are four common styles.

One is to funnel communication *through the therapist,* which takes some of the emotional intensity from disagreements. One person talks to the therapist, who answers; then the other person talks to the therapist, who answers.

Other therapists work with *one spouse at a time* while the other watches. Such therapists may first discuss an issue with the wife for five minutes, while the husband observes; the hope is that the husband will learn new ways to deal with his wife. After a while, the husband will have a similar conversation with the therapist while the wife observes.

Still other therapists have partners talk *directly to each other,* with the therapist interrupting after almost every exchange to clarify or comment on the communication.

Finally, other therapists direct the couple to have longer conversations (a few minutes), and then the therapist might replay the conversation on videotape or audiotape or might discuss the conversation in some detail.

Goals for marital therapy often differ among therapists too. Some prefer to have the couple try to make specific changes, while others are more general, hoping that the couple will improve their communication or be more satisfied. In my experience, the road to major changes in the relationship is almost always through making specific changes.

Often attitude changes occur first and precipitate changes in behavior, but in marriage counseling, where both partners have had extended conflict or unhappiness, this rarely occurs. To change their attitudes, the partners first need to act differently. *Behavioral changes then become the springboard for changes in feelings and attitudes.*

What to Look For
If you decide to seek a counselor, you will want to find someone who can give you the best help possible. Is the therapist a Christian, and what

are his or her beliefs? Has the therapist been recommended by someone you trust? How can you tell if the therapist is competent?

Is the counselor a Christian? Committed Christians may prefer to see a counselor who professes Christianity. A Christian counselor will probably not trample the client's important values and beliefs. It's important to remember, though, that Christian counselors differ substantially in how they counsel. There is no one type of Christian counseling, and clients shouldn't enter counseling expecting the counselor to pray aloud at the beginning of the session, quote Scripture, give sermonettes, use Christian terminology or engage in Christian rituals. While some counselors may do some or all of these things, there are no "Christian counseling techniques" that all Christian therapists use.

What are the counselor's religious beliefs and values? The theological orientation of the counselor may be important. Many Christian counselors seldom use Scripture directly in their counseling, though they may try hard to make sure that their counseling is informed by and consistent with Scripture (or at least not at odds with Scripture).

If Scripture is important in your life and in your spouse's life, and if you tend to justify actions according to verses from the Bible, then the counselor's theological positions and use of Scripture may be important to know. Most secular counselors are not comfortable being questioned about their religious beliefs and values, but most Christian counselors are quite willing to answer questions about their religious beliefs at the beginning of counseling.

In selecting a good counselor, don't be concerned about keeping the counselor comfortable. If particular religious beliefs might prompt you to be more receptive—or more resistant—to counseling, ask. If the counselor is bothered by your straightforward approach, that is good to discover *before* you start counseling.

What is the counselor's experience? While experience is not the sole mark of excellence, experienced therapists are usually better able to help couples than are inexperienced therapists. Degrees, I believe, are less important than the therapist's reputation. I know excellent marital therapists who are clinical psychologists, counseling psychologists, psychiatrists, social workers, licensed professional counselors, pastors, pastoral counselors, rehabilitation counselors and psychiatric nurses. Generally, pastors and other helping professionals have a list of marital therapists to whom they refer. Referrals are usually to be preferred to picking a name from the phone book.

How competent is the therapist? Even more important is how competently the therapist conducts therapy. Can the therapist control hostilities between conflicted marriage partners? Does the therapist grasp the essence of your problem? Does the therapist have an "ax to grind," such as promoting a particular theological position, a particular view of male-female roles, or membership in his or her church? Does the therapist impose his or her values on you, or does the therapist expose those values and respectfully allow you to accept or reject them?

After meeting several times, do you have a good professional relationship with the therapist? A good relationship will be indicated by confidence that the therapist can help you, a feeling that the therapist accepts you and a sense of some hope that progress can be made.

Is the therapist obviously biased toward one of you? No therapist can or *should be* totally unbiased. There are times when a good therapist should side with each of you. Yet a good therapist will usually try to balance the books, siding with each person about equally and not siding with either most of the time. Generally, you should have the impression that the therapist is not on either side but is on the side of your marriage.

What is the counselor's attitude toward divorce? It is probably helpful to know what the therapist thinks about divorce. Many therapists will say that they are not for or against divorce, that they believe it is right for some people and wrong for others. These therapists try to remain objective, and their objectivity is perhaps a strength.

I prefer a more positive position, though. When I do marriage counseling, I fight against divorce with my whole heart. I want the couple to succeed at marriage, and I try my best to help them succeed.

Sadly, some couples' marriages do not work. All counselors who have any experience know that despite the hardest efforts by counselor and partners, marriages fail. In those cases, with pain and tears, I will help the divorcing partners manage their trauma and hurt.

To me, the divorce dilemma is similar to that of helping a depressed patient. I believe God wants us to be happy, joyful and at peace, but some people become depressed. Rather than reject or condemn these people, I want to help ease their pain and restore them to fruitful and faithful living.

Is the counselor's marital status a consideration? The marital status of the counselor is usually *not* important. Many excellent marital counselors are single, divorced or remarried, and many poor marital counselors are happily married. Just as physicians do not need to have cancer to treat patients who have cancer, marital therapists need skill in treatment more than they need a happy marriage themselves.

There are, of course, times when marital status is important—such as when a therapist tries to impose solutions that work in his or her marriage on a couple for whom those solutions would be inappropriate, or when a divorced therapist tries to justify his or her own divorce by unconsciously guiding couples toward divorce. But such difficulties actually reflect the therapist's lack of competence more than his or her marital status.

How About Marriage Enrichment?

If you have examined your marriage closely and have decided that marriage counseling is inappropriate for you, then you might be interested in a marriage enrichment program. There are a variety of these programs with different emphases.

The Association of Couples for Marriage Enrichment (ACME) convenes groups of couples to discuss prescribed topics. Couples don't receive structured information about the topics. Structured Enrichment, developed by Luciano L'Abate, presents each couple with structured information, which they discuss as a couple in the presence of a counselor. Marriage Encounter, the Minnesota Couples Communication Program and the Conjugal Relationship Enhancement Program provide some structured information to couples and ask them to discuss it either in a group or as a couple. Also, many pastors create their own marriage enrichment programs; these may involve a variety of formats—weekly Sunday-school classes, weekly small-group meetings or weekend retreats.

Marriage Encounter is an intense weekend in which couples hear talks and retreat to their rooms to write dialogues about their feelings on an assigned topic. After ten minutes, partners exchange what they have written and read each other's reactions. Emphasis is placed on expressing feelings clearly rather than on resolving differences. As the weekend progresses, the level of intimacy of sharing increases, culminating in a final forty-five-minute written evaluation of the marriage and forty-five minutes of discussion. Marriage is considered to be a striving for spiritual unity, which is subject to deterioration if the couple fails to continue to communicate their feelings. Dialog is believed to repair the erosion of spiritual unity.

Generally, marriage enrichment programs include three building blocks: provision of information about marriage, discussion as a couple and discussion within a group of couples. In a recent study, Beverley Buston, Michael Hammonds and I analyzed the effects of two of these components—information and group discussion.[2] Group discussion was more powerful for increasing couples' intimacy than no group discussion, but information given out in our three sessions of marriage enrichment didn't appreciably affect the couples.

The effectiveness of Marriage Encounter weekends has been studied thoroughly; one such study is by William Doherty, Mary Ellen Lester and their colleagues.[3] These researchers found that most people report positive effects of Marriage Encounter, but about ten percent of the couples who attend Marriage Encounter weekends emerge with more problems than they had when the weekend began. (This does not include the couples who left before the retreat was over, usually due to illness or marital distress.)

In later research, the investigators found that about ten percent of the couples attending Marriage Encounter experienced lasting change. Half of those ten percent got better, and half worse. The remaining couples reported only mild positive changes or no change due to the weekend.

The ten percent reporting lasting change—both positive and negative—were those with the most disturbance in their marriage prior to the weekend. It seems, then, that marriage enrichment can be risky as well as beneficial.

Most negative effects of the weekend were due to one of three causes. In some cases, the dialogues stimulated increased marital conflict. In other cases, increased expression of feelings made the couple more hesitant to discuss other ongoing conflicts out of fear of even more disagreement. Finally, some marriages suffered because the couple became overly enmeshed with each other and the children were excluded, which caused stress in the marriage later.

Overall, marriage enrichment groups can be a good way to get away from the routines of life and build new intimacy. Research on Marriage Encounter, though, suggests that the weekends may be risky for distressed couples, and that nondistressed couples should avoid unrealistic expectations about how much marriage enrichment can help.

Changing Your Own Marriage

Whether you think you could benefit by counseling or whether you have decided not to seek such help, you can change your own marriage. You will be most likely to improve your marriage if you and your spouse work in concert, but you alone can have some positive effects.

All marriages need to change at times. Gardens that are left unattended develop weeds. Similarly, marriages that are not worked on soon sprout weeds that choke love. So we must vigilantly weed and feed the garden of marriage.

When Does Love Grow?

Recall a time when your love for your spouse grew greatly.

For Kirby and me, love grew when we attended a marriage enrichment workshop a few months after we were married. Discussing marital problems and joys with couples of different ages and experiences helped us handle some of the rough times of our first year of marriage and provided positive goals.

Our love seemed to leap ahead during our third summer together. Living north of San Francisco, we camped in various California spots every weekend that summer. Each Friday afternoon, we were off to the wilds to feed a new bunch of hungry mosquitoes.

Our love grew measurably when we traveled together—to Hawaii, to Japan, to Thailand and throughout Europe. We spent four wonderful months in Europe for a thousand dollars in the summer of 1974. Tent camping, surviving on powdered soup and stale bread and meeting new people provided challenges. The joys of seeing the great museums of Europe, spending two weeks at Swiss L'Abri and several days at English L'Abri, and finally going into Paris for a real French meal—at a real restaurant— provided ecstatic memories. The struggles and the memories drew us closer together than ever.

Having children showed us how inadequate and unprepared we were for rearing a family. But in dealing with our inadequacies under God's protection, we drew closer.

During our child-rearing years, the busyness of demanding schedules, careers and children have often sapped our energy, but family camping trips, sharing walks and meals as a couple and taking a country-and-western dance class together have bonded us even more firmly.

As I muse on our twenty-plus years of marriage, I find that it's the breaks from routine that have energized our marriage. The time we laboriously and sacrificially wrenched from our busy schedules to be together has paid dividends. The extra effort of doing new things has kept us fresh.

Change always looks daunting. It requires effort and sacrifice. But in change and freedom from routine, there is growth and renewal. It is imperative, then, that we maintain a positive attitude about change.

5

Preparing
to Change

Most positive change in a mar-
riage doesn't just happen. It occurs by God's grace through the efforts
of a couple who are committed to each other and are willing to risk time
and energy to improve their marriage. In this chapter I identify a dozen
positive attitudes to cultivate as you work to change your marriage.

1. Change Is Worth the Risk
Change is risky.

Whenever you try to change your marriage, you step into the unknown. Things could get better or worse. But if you don't try to improve,
your marriage will almost certainly run downhill. Trying to improve is
usually worth the risk, and you'll accomplish more with an optimistic
attitude toward change than with a pessimistic attitude. Expect and work
for the positive.

2. Change Takes Time and Hard Work

Change can't be willed into existence. And you can't change your marriage simply by reading books, listening to tapes or radio programs or attending conferences and inspirational lectures. Change takes hard work. And time. Marriage is a marathon, not a sprint.

3. Focus on Solutions

When marital problems develop, even if the problems are small, it's natural to try to understand the problems and their causes. But attention to the problem alone, and not to the solution, can mire you in quicksand.

When we learn a new skill, we concentrate on our behavior. Our movements are ragged and uncoordinated. As we practice, though, we become more coordinated.

Problems disrupt our coordination. Thinking that had long been automatic becomes intentional again, and it shouldn't be.

For example, when a child learns to ride a bike, he or she awkwardly concentrates on every action. After a while, though, bike riding becomes automatic. Imagine what would happen if the child suddenly began to think of every movement necessary to ride the bike. Wipe out!

The same may be true with marriage. At first, marriage feels unnatural and uncomfortable. With time, though, partners begin to feel comfortable with each other. If problems develop, though, the marriage can again feel awkward. Like the biker who begins thinking about every little movement, when a couple focuses on their problems, they often create other problems. Rather than focus on the problem, the couple should attend to solving it.

4. Do More of What Works

You have had more experience with your marriage than anyone else has. In that experience, you have undoubtedly found things that work. In troubled marriages, spouses are so focused on problems that they are sometimes reluctant to admit that there are positive interactions hiding beneath the conflict, lack of trust, unforgiveness and separateness. The problems have spread like a blanket over the positive relationship strategies.

A great approach to cultivate is *find the positive and do more of it.* Ask yourself, When was the last time things went well in our marriage? What did we do to make that happen? How did I react to my spouse and my spouse to me? Discuss these memories with your spouse, and try to re-create the positive experiences.

5. Drop the "Motives" Issue

I have never seen a couple actually set out to ruin their marriage. The husband doesn't say, "Well, what dirty, rotten thing can I do to aggravate my wife today?" The wife doesn't say, "Let's see, if I watch soap operas all day instead of doing these jobs, then it will provoke a fight and probably destroy our marriage—which is exactly what I want."

To the contrary, even the most troubled couples sincerely want to have a happy marriage. Who wants unhappiness? Sure, when a spouse has hurt his or her partner repeatedly, a spirit of retaliation can enter the relationship, but most people retaliate only because they want to stop future hostilities, not to escalate the hostilities.

The problem is almost never with motives but with faulty execution. When a wife who has been put down hurts her husband in return, she is usually trying to intimidate him into being nice to her. But the impact she has is not what she intended. Instead, her husband returns hurt for hurt, as he tries to force his wife to be more considerate. Both spouses are trying to improve the relationship, but they're going about it ineffectively. The exchange of coercive communications only drives the wedge further between the partners.

Even worse, if you imagine that your spouse wants only to destroy your marriage, that casts a negative light on every interaction between you, even when some of them are positive.

6. Focus on Your Own Behavior

Everyone wants to understand what causes marital problems, and so our natural tendency is to explain problems in light of what we observe. What do we observe? Our spouse's behavior.

Listen as Natalie explains her problems to her friend, Jane. "I got angry because Lonnie criticized me. I just couldn't stand it anymore. He came in and threw his sport coat across the sofa, and he had the nerve to yell at *me*, 'This place looks like a dump. Don't you do anything all day except lie around and watch the soaps?' I mean, who is he to accuse me of slacking off? He's so glued to the tube during football season that all he does is talk in grunts. If he can waste all that time watching the Redskins on television, how come I can't watch two soaps a day?"

Natalie blames her husband for their problems because she sees *his* behavior. It is hard to examine her own behavior objectively. Yet if she and Lonnie are going to break free of their negative cycles of blame and anger, Natalie must change her own behavior.

As long as Natalie and Lonnie blame each other for their problems, they are doomed to complain about them. At best, they can only hope to change each other, and that is not likely to happen. Attempts to reform a spouse will usually be resisted, especially if an ongoing power struggle is being waged.

To improve their marriage, Natalie and Lonnie—or at least one of the two—must take responsibility for changing their own behavior more positively. Once each begins to see that the other person is voluntarily changing, change will be easier for both of them.

7. Be the First to Change

Natalie and Lonnie have tumbled into one of the traps that clutch at partners who would like to improve their marriage. Lonnie says, "I've tried and tried to change our marriage, and it hasn't done any good. I don't believe Natalie really wants to change. I'm not going to put myself on the line again until I have concrete evidence that she is willing to change."

Lonnie will probably have to wait a long time. Once he has accepted a negative view of the marriage, he won't see how Natalie is trying to improve. He must forget about Natalie's behavior and concentrate on making the first move, even if he feels he has made the first move a hundred times before.

8. Try to Work Together

If you can work together, you are more likely to make productive and lasting changes in your marriage. Marriage counseling done with both spouses together is substantially more likely to result in an improved marriage than will counseling partners individually or counseling only one partner.

Yet even if your spouse doesn't agree to work on your marriage, you can still help your marriage. When you try to be more open, promote more closeness, communicate better, resolve conflict more productively, avoid blaming your partner and exhibit renewed commitment, your partner can sense those efforts and may respond in kind.

9. Be Patient with Your Spouse

Couples caught in a rut have almost an ant's-eye view of the future. Their experience trying to change their marriage is like that of the ant as it tries to escape its rut.

The ant can see clearly only as it looks down a seemingly never-ending rut. It hurries along this path but gains no altitude. It has difficulty seeing the green pastures that begin only inches outside the rut. To get out of the rut, the ant has to reach the edge of the rut, where it begins to gain elevation. As it begins to climb the steep sides, it exerts great energy. At first, the work is laborious, and little progress is seen because the slope is so steep at the bottom of the rut. As the ant nears the top, though, the rut flattens out, and suddenly new vistas open before the ant's eyes. It's a bit like Dorothy opening her gray Kansas door to a vividly colored Land of Oz.

Similarly, partners in a stagnant marriage feel trapped. All they can see is more of the same humdrum boredom. They decide to change, but at first seem to be getting nowhere. Finally, change begins to occur, but it is difficult. Each three steps forward are followed by two (and sometimes three or four) backward. This uneven progress tests the permanence of change and the partners' commitment to changing the marriage. Usually, it tests their patience too. After much work, though, progress actually becomes visible, until new arenas of freedom are opened to the couple. Through it all, patience and faith are the sustaining virtues.

Sometimes changing your marriage can be like riding a roller coaster: there are mechanical creaks and groans as the heavy carriage strains uphill, followed by breathtaking plunges, headsnapping turns and head-over-heels loop-de-loops. When it feels this way, comfort yourself that you are not on a merry-go-round.

10. Don't Expect Perfection

"Well, nobody expects perfection," you say. In the abstract, we all agree that no one is perfect, yet many people live as if they expected perfection from themselves or their spouses. A perfectionist attitude often crops up when couples are having the most difficult times with their marriage. When the relationship is sailing along smoothly, all sorts of sins, mistakes, blunders, criticisms and unintentional (and even intentional) insults wash over us like clean water in a swimming pool. When partners get hurt and their sensitivity is raised, even the slightest criticism sticks like muddy goo to new clothes.

When trying to improve your marriage, you must swim against the natural current. Focus on successes rather than attuning yourself to the negative. That requires a conscious decision and willful attention to the positive. It also involves a willingness to ignore any negative. Don't discuss the negative. Try not to even think about it.

11. Look to God

God wants your marriage not only to survive but also to mirror the joy of the spiritual relationship between Christ and the church (Eph 5:25-33) and between the believer and Jesus (1 Cor 6:16-17). When a marriage is attacked from within or without, it is an indication of spiritual warfare.

Paul, in his letter to the Ephesians, gives a powerful summary of his main points throughout the letter in his admonishment to "put on the whole armor of God, so that you may be able to stand against the wiles of the devil" (Eph 6:11). We can apply this armor to all our relationships, including our marriages.

The first weapon in the married couple's armory is truth (6:14). It's important to remember that truth is to be spoken in love (4:15) rather than used as a weapon of pain and hurt against the spouse. Further, truth is to be spoken to build us into unity with Christ (4:15-16).

Next, spouses are to put on the breastplate of righteousness (6:14). Putting off their old nature (4:22) characterized by the idolatry of covetousness (5:5), sexual impropriety (5:3) and hurtful, disrespectful or deceitful talk (5:4, 6), they are to put on their new nature of righteousness. Despite the temptations, they are to be imitators of God, walking in sacrificial love for each other (5:1-2).

The gospel of peace should shine from the marriage (6:15). Others should be drawn to Christianity because of the peace they see in the Christian couple. Paul says, "I therefore, the prisoner in the Lord, beg you to lead a life worthy of the calling to which you have been called, with all humility and gentleness, with patience, bearing with one another in love, making every effort to maintain the unity of the Spirit in the bond of peace" (4:1-3). Interestingly, he places peace within a context of love and forgiveness, the soul of marriage.

The shield of faith in Christ specifically protects us from spiritual attack (6:16). Throughout Ephesians, Paul stresses the unity of the faith—something Christians share despite the doctrines that divide and the interpersonal frictions that grate on us. That unity of faith within the marriage is necessary to defeat the attacks of Satan.

Salvation (6:17) is our induction into God's army. Membership in God's army is the partners' primary allegiance, but they find that their loyalty to their unit (the marriage—and later the family) grows as they make mutual sacrifices on behalf of the Lord.

God's Word, the sword of the Spirit (6:17), gives us guidelines about our life together within the bonds of marriage and the unity of the church. Those guidelines are one source of our vision of marriage, which undergirds our entire approach to marriage and provides a worthy goal for our efforts.

Frank Peretti has heightened our awareness of the vital role of prayer in spiritual warfare through his bestselling novels *This Present Darkness* and *Piercing the Darkness*.[1] Prayer, one of our primary spiritual weapons, is vital to the marriage relationship; partners who try to strengthen their marriage without relying on God's leadership and power are in for a struggle (6:18).

12. Get Down to Specifics

If you want to make your marriage better, where do you start? Begin with specific assessments of the six fundamental areas of marriage: confession and forgiveness, closeness, communication, conflict resolution, causal attributions and commitment. Each of the following six chapters deals with a separate area. In each chapter, you will assess your relationship, mark your assessment on a "Marriage Thermometer" (see figure 2) and read about ways you can change your marriage if it needs modification in the area dealt with in the chapter. Whether your marriage changes depends on whether you and your spouse actually try to change your behavior in each area.

Don't try to fill in the "Marriage Thermometers" now. You will return to them after making an assessment in each chapter.

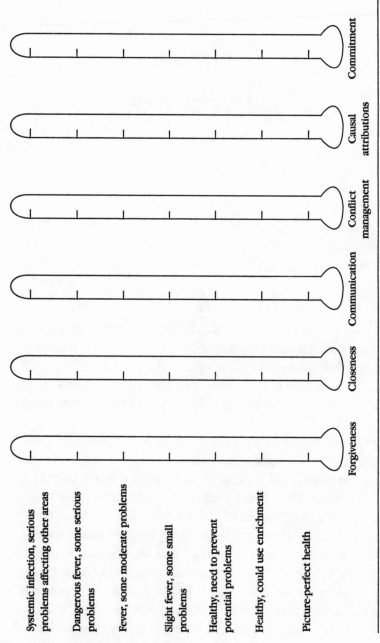

Figure 2. Take your marriage's temperature by completing each thermometer.

6

Confession and Forgiveness

At the center of every successful marriage is each spouse's capacity and willingness to confess his or her inadequacies and to ask for forgiveness. The flip side of this crucial element of marriage is each partner's capacity and willingness of each partner to forgive the other—regardless of whether the partner asks for forgiveness.

Confession is each person's sincere recognition of his or her part in marital tensions. Willingness to confess is not martyred affliction or self-absorption in guilt and depression. Such attitudes would bespeak attempts to manipulate others through guilt or pity. Rather, confession is a paradox: an abandonment of self-centeredness and self-justification and an acceptance of personal responsibility for actions and decisions.

Forgiveness is an attitude of the heart, enabling one to cease blaming the spouse for hurts inflicted intentionally or unintentionally. Forgiveness is not saying an unsolicited "I forgive you" to the spouse who offends, for this sort of statement covertly blames the spouse. When the spouse has not sought forgiveness, "I forgive you" is often interpreted as "You need forgiveness because you have done wrong."

True forgiveness is an attitude, a decision not to hold the spouse's actions against him or her. It is an honest attempt to forget wrongs, separating negative evaluations of the spouse's actions from one's feelings—as far as east is from west (Ps 103:12).

Naturally, when a marriage is working well, one spouse's confession will usually be followed by verbal reassurance of forgiveness. Such assurance of forgiveness, when prompted by confession, fosters freedom and reassurance within the marriage rather than blame.

Sincere confession, true forgiveness and assurance of forgiveness are the keys that open the gates to the other aspects of healthy marriage—closeness, communication, conflict resolution and causal attributions—and these in turn lead to contentment, which strengthens commitment.

Confessing and forgiving attitudes encourage each spouse to be vulnerable to and trusting of the other. This bond leads to emotional and sexual closeness. Confession and forgiveness open the path for communication, baring the inner self with assurance that each lover's pearls will not be trampled on. Confession and forgiveness make conflict resolution possible. Differences of opinion inevitably lead to misunderstandings and pain, but if each spouse can be assured that the other will accept responsibility for his or her own mistakes and harms and will also be tolerant of inflicted harm, then differences can be discussed with openness and sensitivity. Confession and forgiveness help each partner maintain a positive attitude about the other. There is mutual confidence that both partners are working hard to enjoy a healthy marriage rather than working hard to protect the self. Confession and forgiveness glue the marriage components together.

Assessing Confession and Forgiveness

In chapter four, you assessed your satisfaction with your marriage. Improvement in marriage depends on identifying specific areas in which to make changes. In this chapter and those that follow, you will examine your marriage in six major areas. Depending on your self-evaluation, you may conclude that improvement is needed in certain areas but perhaps not in other areas. Each chapter suggests ways you can change your relationship. If your relationship seems satisfactory in a particular area, skip the suggestions and go on to the following chapter. Remember, write the answers to the highlighted questions.

Grab paper and a pencil and give honest answers.

☐ Examine yourself. How willing are you to say, "I was wrong"?

☐ Can you admit your mistakes, or do you usually cover them up?

☐ If you are able to admit your mistakes and the things you have done to harm your spouse, are you free from manipulative intent, or do you confess to get something from your spouse (such as a reciprocal confession, or sympathy, or attention)?

☐ How willing are you to forgive when your spouse does something that hurts you?

☐ Do you use forgiveness as a punishment?

☐ Is your forgiveness spontaneous and from the heart?

☐ Are you able to truly put aside past hurts, or do you dwell on them, especially at night in the "late-late show" reruns of the mind?

☐ How willing is your spouse to confess his or her faults to you?

☐ Are you able to let your spouse be an individual in this regard without trying to change him or her?

☐ How willing is your spouse to forgive you when you ask for forgiveness?

☐ Do you sense that your spouse holds grudges? If so, can you truly forgive your spouse in your heart for that?

Having considered confession and forgiveness within your marriage, go back to figure 2 (at the end of chapter five) and assess the health of your relationship in this area. Mark your assessment directly on figure 2.

Lessons About Confession

Remember Danielle and Gus from chapter one?

Like all couples, Danielle and Gus have had their problems over their thirty-two years of marriage. They think of themselves as "stickers" because of their commitment to each other through long separations caused by military service and personal hardships such as unemployment.

But commitment alone would not have kept Danielle and Gus as involved with each other as they are. When I interviewed them, they gazed at each other like high-school lovers.

"What gives you such obvious love for each other?" I asked.

Danielle, always the more vocal of the two, said, "We respect each other." She looked at Gus, then continued. "Gus really lets me know that he thinks I'm a worthwhile person. When we're together I feel like a queen. At least I think we have a great mutual respect. What do you think, honey?"

"Sex all the time," said Gus. He looked at Danielle. Her jaw dropped in shock. "That always gets a rise out of her." Gus threw back his head and laughed.

Danielle pushed Gus's arm with both of her hands. "Be serious," she said.

"Well, we don't have sex *all* the time," he relented. "I guess one reason we have a good relationship is that we laugh a lot and look at the bright side of life. We've always emphasized our strengths more than our faults."

I leaned forward. "Let me follow up. You emphasize the positive side of your marriage. You seem to be saying that if you keep a positive focus, you won't have problems. Yet earlier you said you've had some troubles. How did you handle those troubles?"

Danielle leaned forward; her energy and enthusiasm were apparent. "We keep a short account with each other. If anything goes wrong, like if I say something stupid or act inconsiderate, I apologize right away. I don't want those negative things to build up. They take too much fun out of life if you worry about them."

"So how do you make up when something negative does occur?" I said.

Danielle said, "We do things for each other to try to make it up, and of course we say we're sorry right off the bat."

Gus reached his arm around Danielle and gave her a squeeze. "We just believe in putting each other first. If we hurt each other, then we need to make it right and not wait for the other one to come and beg."

Gus and Danielle made a two-pronged assault on their troubles: they focused on the good parts of their relationship and took care of problems instantly. Their attitude of being quick to forgive and not keeping track of who hurt whom last or most is an excellent strategy for any marriage.

Jay and Monica were dealing with different life stresses from Gus and Danielle's. They had been married for twelve years. "We have three kids, two dogs, a mortgage and 136 plastic Teenage Mutant Ninja Turtles—all of which are undoubtedly the joys of our lives."

Monica was an active mom, working part-time as a secretary, participating in PTA and Girl Scouts and transporting her children to several youth sporting events each week. She was attractive and conscious of her looks. I never saw her without her hair fixed and lipstick in place. She had a dry sense of humor; her witty, sometimes cynical comments invariably caught me off guard.

Jay was a perfect counterpart for her. He was also active, involved in coaching a youth soccer team and volunteering his services on several community-service boards. He was always friendly, and he had a naive openness that made him a perfect foil for Monica's cynical quips. He seemed to delight in her and frequently laughed at her remarks.

"I'm interviewing couples for my book to find out how they deal with some of their trials," I said.

"That's exactly what I love to talk about—my dirty laundry," said Monica. "Sure, ask anything. Go ahead. Make my day."

Jay crossed his legs. "We've definitely had our tough times. We're even having some now. But overall, I'd say we've managed okay."

"Only a few flesh wounds. The other scars are internal," Monica inserted. "Still, we're holding together, just trying to survive this stressful stage of life without developing heart disease, cancer or computer addiction."

"How well are you succeeding?" I said.

Jay squirmed into a more comfortable position. "We get on each other's nerves a little." He paused.

"What happens then?" I said.

"We sometimes bark at each other. I usually have a shorter fuse than Monica. She lets her tensions out with humor."

". . . Which is always greatly and enthusiastically appreciated, I might add," Monica broke in. "Actually, sometimes humor wears thin on Jay, and we fuss at each other for a few days. But we bounce back."

I said to Monica, "How do you manage to bounce back? It seems as if you have some strains in your relationship and you're trying to prevent the little torn places from widening."

Monica said, "I'm pretty good at just blocking out the negative. I distract myself, sometimes with more action than I can handle. I'm not very successful at saying to myself, 'Don't think about the negative.' For me, that is like saying, 'Don't think about clowns.' Then I think about clowns just because I tried not to. But I'm pretty good at keeping busy."

"Of course, periodically it catches up with her," interjected Jay. "She gets moody, sometimes for several days. Then it's no fun to be around her. Basically, she's a pill."

"Ouch," said Monica.

"Sorry," said Jay.

"That's something we didn't mention," said Monica. "It's called a pinch. When we get short with each other, we sometimes snipe a little with digs and zingers. Each one is like getting pinched. The person who is pinched has several ways to deal with a pinch." She ticked them off on her fingers. "One, we could let it go and try to forget it. Two, we could let it go and say 'ouch,' acknowledging the pinch but not making a big deal out of it. Three, we could stop and talk about it. Four, we could store up the pinches until we have a boatload and then bring all of them out at once and clobber the other person. But that doesn't exactly contribute to marital bliss, as we have discovered in years past."

"I noticed that this time you just said 'ouch,' " I said, "but, Jay, you responded."

"Of course, that's not required when she says 'ouch,' but we've found—again by trial and error—that it's best to apologize right away even though it isn't required. It saves a lot of hard feelings later."

Talking to Jay and Monica felt different from interviewing Gus and

Danielle. Gus and Danielle seemed to have a vast reservoir of positive experiences that they frequently and naturally drew from. Monica and Jay, though, always seemed to be treading on eggshells. I had the feeling that a wrong word or misdirected gesture was likely to be challenged. The couple who want to prevent problems, then, would be well advised to build up their reservoir of positive experiences and focus on them.

Moreover, Gus and Danielle had few opportunities to repent, but when the opportunities occurred, each was eager to make amends for hurting each other. With Jay and Monica, though, repentance seemed to be more intentional and planned. They first identified clearly what they were doing that was offensive. Then, they tried to stop doing the offensive act. Further, they announced to the other their intention to steer clear of the hurtful act in the future. Finally, they tried to replace the act with some behavior more edifying to their relationship.

Steps Through Forgiveness

Healing a relationship that has been wounded seriously and repeatedly—such as Steve and Doris's marriage, in which there was infidelity and unforgiveness—requires an even more intentional strategy.

Let me suggest a step-by-step procedure to help you walk through healing of hurts and unforgiveness.

1. Conviction. Each person must become convicted that he or she is doing wrong. The Holy Spirit convicts us of sin. Sometimes, in marriages characterized by hurt, partners feel they must help the Holy Spirit along by pointing out each other's sin. Usually, this produces not conviction but defensiveness and hostility. Forgiveness becomes even harder. Rather than become our spouse's prosecutor, we can become his or her advocate before Jesus Christ, praying for the spouse rather than praying against his or her sins.

2. Self-examination. Rather than focus on our spouse's shortcomings, we must focus on our own. In most troubled relationships, each partner is doing plenty of things that contribute to the tension.

The road to reconciliation is paved with self-examination before God, not condemnation. When we honestly examine our own lives before

God, we will find more than enough needed improvements to occupy our attention. Unforgiveness of your spouse is as serious a sin in God's eyes as whatever the spouse has done to offend you. Work on your forgiving attitude.

3. Stop the negative. With God's help, resolve to stop negative behavior. Don't worry about your spouse's behavior; that isn't your responsibility. Take responsibility for your own behavior.

Tell your spouse that you intend to stop acting negatively. Of course, such an announcement is risky, because it leaves you open to criticism when you fail—as you will almost inevitably do at times. But if you are serious about changing your behavior, you'll be more likely to succeed if you make your intentions public than if you keep your intentions secret.

4. Replace the negative with positive. If you merely strive to stop some objectionable behavior, you may succeed. But nature abhors a vacuum. If you do not replace the hurtful behavior with something positive, then more negative behavior is likely to be sucked into the void.

Jesus told of a man delivered from an evil spirit who did not fill the void with the Holy Spirit. Seven other foul spirits soon harassed the man. Similarly, the troubled marriage must replace negative aspects with positive, preferably by using a specific plan. Ask, How can I promote healing in this area? Then set a goal and strive for it.

5. Cue cards. Although actors memorize their parts, the stress of performance sometimes rattles even the most seasoned veterans. Through trial and error, cue cards were developed to help actors past the rough parts.

When you are trying to confess your shortcomings more honestly and forgive more sincerely, set up your environment to cue you. For instance, if you've been critical and want to replace that with praise, use the word *praise* as a cue to praise your spouse. You could thus play a *praise* album in your car stereo on the way home from work, sing a *praise* song to God just before your spouse arrives home, or place a blank piece of paper in your coffee cup so you see it first thing in the morning as a reminder to *praise* your spouse.

Using cues will help you change patterns of criticism and unforgiveness, but cues quickly lose their effectiveness. Employ cues only a few days. Then change the cues. Keep using new cues until the new patterns become habitual. Building new habits may take weeks, even months. Even then it is easy to slide back into old habits.

When you try to change old patterns, you are undertaking one of the most difficult tasks a person can face. High motivation and good intentions will usually keep you going for a few days. Using cues may help you maintain your efforts longer.

Dealing with Your Failures

Making permanent changes takes constant effort and vigilance. At times, you will probably fail. How can you deal with failure?

☐ Say, "It wasn't meant to be," and give up trying to change.

☐ Say, "I failed. This is terrible. I'm such a jerk. I think I'll just go live in a cave and eat worms."

☐ Get angry with your spouse, children or busy schedule for making you fail.

☐ Vow never to forgive yourself for the weakness of character that has kept you from being totally forgiving.

☐ Doubt God's power to effect real, lasting changes in your life.

☐ Say, "It doesn't matter at all whether I succeed. This isn't important."

☐ Say, "Wow, was Worthington stupid to recommend trying to change this!"

While all these coping methods have their own allure, and all release you from the effort of trying to change and the pain of future failures, none of them is very helpful if you really want to improve your marriage.

Rather, cultivate an attitude toward yourself that is not condemning, one that allows you to hurdle your failure and keep running toward a better marriage. In short, forgive yourself and seek God's forgiveness too.

Examine your motivations and confess wrong motivations to God. Repent of future failure, and declare your resolve to succeed with God's help. Ask for God's help, and his forgiveness. Seek to repair the break your failure has caused in your relationship with your spouse.

Dealing with Your Spouse's Failures

Unfortunately, your spouse will also fail at times. If your marriage has been troubled for some time, you will then probably be tempted to think, "See, I knew he (or she) wasn't serious about trying to make things better. This proves it." You might even think, "I knew it was impossible to change. Our marriage is hopeless."

If a man were being sucked into quicksand, you wouldn't toss him a heavy weight. The weight would simply drag him down faster. Both of these thoughts have the same effect on the marriage as tossing a weight to the man up to his neck in quicksand.

Rather, take the same forgiving attitude toward your spouse's failures as toward your own. Listen to his or her confession with respect, and avoid gloating. Even if your spouse doesn't admit failures to you, keep a positive attitude. Think, "I know he [or she] is trying. He wants our marriage to succeed." Think, "No one's perfect. I fail too." Be tolerant and forgiving, even if it seems as if you've forgiven a million times before. Remember, progress is like a roller coaster, not a steady uphill climb.

Dealing with Your Spouse's Successes

A marriage under stress is like a toothache. A toothache doesn't hurt all the time; we just think it does. We don't expect our teeth to cause pain, so when one hurts, we think about it frequently, and at the end of the day, we say that it hurt all day.

We tend to think that a marriage should never hurt. When we develop a "marriage ache," we too easily forget about or don't even notice anything positive that the spouse does. This must change.

Plan to pay special attention to the nice things your spouse does, and comment on them in such a way as to reward your spouse.

One couple in counseling undertook a program of "caring days," in which they tried to do one nice thing for each other daily. But the husband would "reward" his wife by saying, "Well, *finally* you're doing something besides think about yourself." Needless to say, she did not feel very rewarded by such a backhanded compliment. Sincerely appreciate your spouse. Don't use "compliments" as an occasion to remind him or her of past failures.

Handling Success as a Couple

Rewards are not important in themselves, and we certainly do not want to work to improve our marriage simply to obtain rewards. But rewards serve as trophies signifying that we are progressing toward a goal. We all need rewards when we succeed.

With your spouse, consider allocating some money each week to reward your progress toward improving your marriage. For instance, one couple enjoyed eating out, but while their children were young, they had stopped eating out to save money on food and babysitting. After their children got old enough to care for themselves, however, the couple set aside one night a week to eat out—usually taking advantage of a "special" at one of the local restaurants.

What if expected progress doesn't come about? When expectations are not met, it's natural to blame someone—usually the spouse. You'll find it more productive, though, to take stock of why the changes have not occurred. Then change the goals and the methods of trying to reach them, so they can be reached.

Rebuild Trust

When trust has been seriously violated by one or both partners, the question always arises, "How much evidence is enough for trust to be reestablished?" The person who violated the trust wants instant forgiveness, based on the assurance that "it'll never happen again." The other person feels reluctant to forgive: "It happened once. It can happen again."

Trust cannot be granted instantly. While the offended person may forgive, the breach in trust may take a long while to heal. A violation of trust is like a compound fracture, which requires that the bone be set, the area be kept free of infection and proper treatment be applied during the period of healing.

That does not mean that the offended person can hold the transgression over the other person's head indefinitely. When Dwayne and Sandra came for counseling, Sandra had just extricated herself from an affair. Penitently, she claimed she had learned her lesson, confessed her sin and promised never again to break her marital pledge. When Dwayne expressed reservations, she had become indignant. Their disagreements had brought them to counseling.

Usually, in such serious violations of marital trust as sexual infidelity, I ask the offended party to set a specific date and specific conditions under which he or she will declare that trust has "officially" been reestablished. I made this request of Dwayne, who said that Sandra must give good evidence of marital devotion for at least a year.

Although Dwayne couldn't completely control his *feelings* and simply turn them on or off on a particular day, he could control his *behavior*. After a year, Dwayne had no suspicions about Sandra's faithfulness. Thus, since his conditions had been met, Dwayne followed through on his part of the agreement: never to bring up the transgression again and to *act as if* it had never happened.

After four years Dwayne and Sandra returned to counseling for an unrelated matter: dealing with an unruly teenager. They spontaneously volunteered an update on their earlier agreement. Dwayne reported that after a period of acting as if the affair had never occurred, he realized one day that he actually did trust Sandra and truly believed that she would remain faithful.

Summary

Let's summarize.

If forgiveness has been a problem area in your marriage, here are some things to remember.

☐ Be quicker to confess your own faults than to point an accusing finger at your partner.

☐ Don't dwell on the failures; set positive goals and work toward them.

☐ Try not to repeat past failures.

☐ Ask for and accept God's help.
☐ Reward yourselves as a couple when you succeed.
☐ Let trust grow over time.

7

Closeness

Life is full of tensions. We desire oneness with God, but we need to be individuals. God is one, yet the Godhead is a trinity—Father, Son and Holy Spirit. Jesus was fully human, yet fully God. We have free will, yet God is in total control of existence. Our understanding of these tensions is taxed, and our lives are like tightrope walks, balancing between two sides of truths that seem conflicting.

Larry Christenson once described God's truth as being like a hula hoop—unified and whole.[1] Our mind is like a matchbox. Our mind is too small to fully contain God's truth; the hula hoop won't fit into the matchbox. So God cuts the hula hoop and inserts each end into a different side of our mind. As a consequence, we see what appears to be opposites. If we could see from God's perspective, however, we would recognize the truths as unified.

The needs for intimacy and individuality are each side of one of the tightropes we walk. We each have a different balance point for intimacy, distance and coaction. Like tightrope walkers, we have a comfort zone within which we can remain balanced. If we fall outside the comfort zone, we lose our balance and risk tumbling to the ground.

Marriage is an important way we meet our needs for intimacy, aloneness and working together—for achieving balanced closeness. But achieving and maintaining our balance requires continual adjustments as we are buffeted by changing life circumstances, our own stresses and each other's reactions to stress.

Mario and Kathleen experienced such a struggle.

Tensions in Closeness

Here we go again, thought Mario as he looked into Kathleen's eyes brimming with tears. The left corner of her top lip was quivering—a sure sign that she was going to cry. *Why does this always seem to happen when the pressure is greatest? Why can't she have these crying times when I'm not under such stress?*

"I just need to be held," said Kathleen, in what Mario had come to think of as her wounded-puppy manner.

No, you don't, thought Mario angrily. *You need to take up our entire night, and I need the time.* He folded his arms around her and felt her sobs begin.

After a while, Mario sighed and pulled back, but Kathleen held on, as if Mario were a lifeline and she were adrift in a cold sea. He sighed again and patted her back reassuringly.

Kathleen clung desperately to Mario, wanting to hold his body close to hers to draw strength from him. *Nobody really cares for me except Mario,* she thought. *I haven't a real friend in the world. Just acquaintances. Without Mario, I'd die.* She sobbed again, and as if a dam had broken, the tears streamed down her face. "I need you," she said, watching the tears wet his collar.

"I need you too," his answer came back softly.

She sensed his support but also his frustration. *I wish I didn't depend so much on his support. I wish I could stand on my own two feet. I know it drives him crazy when I get this way, but I can't help it. I just don't know anywhere else to turn.* "I feel so rejected. Sarah and Jaime said they would help me with this big project at church, but now both of them have backed out. I have to do all of it, and with everything else going on, I just don't see how. But it's the rejection that bothers me the most . . ."

Kathleen's spate of words had begun, and true to Mario's expectations, it would continue into the night while he listened patiently. Locked into a cycle, Kathleen and Mario alternated between intimacy and distance as if they were connected by rubber bands. During their alone times, each partner pursued his or her busy life. Under stress, though, Kathleen coped by seeking emotional support, while Mario withdrew from personal contact to manage the crisis efficiently. When only one experienced stress, things worked well, but when both were under stress at the same time, they had mixed emotions.

Kathleen resented her dependency on Mario, and Mario resented the intrusion into his stress-management strategy. Yet Kathleen liked the intimacy and felt warm and cared for. Mario, too, felt needed and valued. The bittersweetness of their crises kept them from changing.

Types of Closeness

At least five types of closeness have been identified by David Olson and Mark Schaefer from the University of Minnesota.[2] They developed a questionnaire to assess those types of intimacy: emotional, sexual, social, intellectual and recreational. Each partner answers questions about how the relationship is perceived *really* to be and how each partner would like it *ideally* to be.

Figure 3 plots an example. One hundred points is considered to be perfect closeness for each area. On the figure, the wife's ratings are connected by dotted lines, while the husband's ratings are connected by solid lines.

Emotional closeness is the amount of emotional connection the spouses feel with each other. It involves empathy, openness of emotional expression, shared feelings about common events, feelings of being understood and appreciated by the partner, absence of feelings of loneliness and a feeling of emotional connectedness.

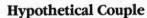

Hypothetical Couple

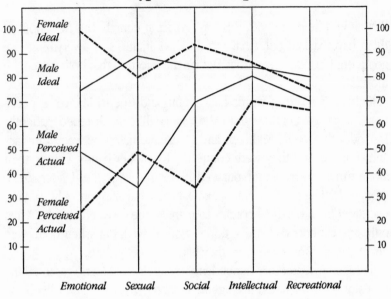

Your Own Rating

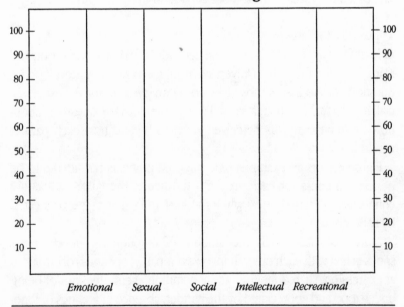

Figure 3. Ratings of Closeness (adapted from PAIR Profile, Schaefer and Olson).

Sexual closeness is a feeling that the couple communicates well sexually. It involves satisfaction with the amount of sexual contact, the frequency of lovemaking, the duration of lovemaking and the types of activities done while making love. It also involves compatibility in communicating about sexual topics.

Social closeness involves the enjoyment the partners feel when spending time together in social situations. It involves essential agreement about the frequency, duration and nature of social activities that are engaged in. Couples with high social closeness may be either outgoing or introverted.

Intellectual closeness is the ability to relate to each other on approximately the same intellectual level. The couple is usually able to share thoughts with neither partner feeling threatened or put down. The partners are able to accept each other's ideas as valid without frequently trying to change those ideas through argumentation or persuasion.

Recreational closeness implies that the couple enjoys being together in recreational settings. Not every activity needs to be done in common, but couples should feel that their lifestyles fit together smoothly and that several recreational interests are held in common.

In the top part of figure 3, I graphed the five types of intimacy for a hypothetical couple. The female holds extremely high ideals for emotional closeness but feels that she has little. Her husband expects less emotional closeness and feels that he receives just a little less than he would like to have. The husband experiences more discrepancy between ideal and perceived actual sexual closeness, while the wife expects less sexual closeness and feels that she experiences more of this type of closeness than the husband. In social closeness, the husband finds the couple to be at nearly an ideal level, but the wife is quite dissatisfied. The two partners essentially agree on intellectual and recreational closeness; although these ratings do not match perfectly, they are close enough that there is essentially no difference.

Now, use the bottom half of figure 3 to estimate the ideal and perceived real intimacy for each of the five types of closeness for your marriage. It would be best if both you and your spouse made estimates on the same graph (using different-colored pens).

If your spouse cannot make the ratings, you might guess at his or her ratings, merely to see how your views of closeness might compare. Once both your and your spouse's ratings are complete, try to think about what the discrepancies mean for your relationship. Based on your assessment, you might target improvement in the areas of closeness where you most differ from your partner.

Now that you have considered types of marital closeness, return to figure 2 (in chapter five) and rate your closeness with your spouse on the Marriage Thermometer.

Dealing with Intimacy Problems

Problems in closeness may be prevented and alleviated by following four strategies: keep the marriage fresh, keep the emotional climate pleasant, anticipate stressful life events and keep time schedules in balance. These are especially helpful for handling problems in social, intellectual and recreational intimacy. After I discuss these four general strategies, I will give special attention to handling problems in emotional and sexual intimacy.

Keeping Marriage Fresh

This summer, I taught a course in effective behavior at Virginia Commonwealth University. I asked the nineteen students in the class to describe ways to improve a marriage. Then I organized their responses, indicating where more than one person made a particular suggestion. I divided their responses into two tables—table 2, which I will discuss here, and table 3, which I'll discuss in the following chapter.

A principal theme of the students' suggestions was to keep the marriage fresh. For example, they recommended taking "minivacations," surprising the spouse, doing nice things for the spouse, being spontaneous and escaping from routines to enjoy life together.

Continuing the theme of freshness in intimate activities, here are some other activities that promote spontaneity.

☐ Make up a progressive story together.

☐ Laugh together and enjoy each other's company. This may involve renting humorous videos, reading joke books together or creating your own jokes.

☐ Act silly. I enjoy catching Kirby while she is undressing and "attacking" her playfully.

It is important to keep your sex life vibrant too. Often when couples have a pleasant sexual relationship, they fall into mutually pleasing routines. Routine adds comfort, but a few small changes might make the sex life even better. In changing lovemaking routines, avoid dramatic changes and make sure that you both fully agree to the new sexual adventures. Books about sex might provide creative ideas about lovemaking. The partners might also involve their fantasies in their lovemaking, perhaps with one pretending to be a masseuse or an anatomy instructor. The fantasy should be playful, humorous, in good taste and enjoyed by both partners.

One husband knew that his wife would be home for lunch. He drove forty minutes from his office to his home, bringing candy and flowers, so they could have a surprise "nooner" while the children were in school.

A Pleasant Emotional Climate

Sharing pleasant activities throughout the week can build a positive emotional atmosphere. Therapists have created some excellent ways to build positive experiences into the normal schedule. For example, spouses may each make up a "wish list" of positive activities. A third list contains activities that the couple enjoys doing together. Items may include taking a bubble bath, eating a chocolate bar, going out to eat, receiving a massage or footrub, having time to read or even having the spouse care for the children for a short period. Each spouse gets a copy of all three lists. Other pleasant activities may be added to any list as they are recalled or invented.

Couples may then alternate "caring days," an idea that has been suggested by Richard Stuart.[3] On caring days, each spouse does one thing from the partner's list. One day each week, partners do an activity they both enjoy.

Table 2. Suggestions for improving intimacy in your marriage.

Create a Positive Relationship

Trust in God

Take the Initiative
- ☐ Think of what *you* can do to improve the relationship; don't wait for the spouse to initiate change

Laugh Together (3)

Sex Life
- ☐ Put excitement into your romance and sex life

Keep the Marriage Fresh
- ☐ Go on mini-vacations to break out of routines
- ☐ Don't get locked into rigid routines (2)

Show Love, Respect and Support

Support and Respect Spouse
- ☐ Support each other (3)
- ☐ Respect the other's dreams, hopes and interests (5)
- ☐ Respect each other's privacy (2)
- ☐ Don't look at another woman unless you have a death wish
- ☐ Try to put yourself in your partner's shoes
- ☐ Don't pry into an area that your partner doesn't want to talk about
- ☐ Don't put your partner down or cuss at him
- ☐ Think, "Is this going to upset her?" or "Will she take it the wrong way?" before acting
- ☐ Make sure material needs are satisfied
- ☐ Always be there for each other
- ☐ Avoid bad habits like drugs and alcohol

Do Something for Your Spouse
- ☐ Surprise your spouse by doing something nice for him or her
- ☐ Help your spouse get work done when he or she is under pressure
- ☐ Take time to do something special for each other
- ☐ At least once a week, cook a meal for your spouse
- ☐ Do special things like send flowers periodically

Be Willing to Give of Yourself
- ☐ Make sacrifices

Share

Share Friends
□ Mutual friends (2)
□ Be involved with each other's family and friends

Share Beliefs
□ Find and share core beliefs

Share Time
□ Spend more time together if you're drifting apart and less time together if you're aggravating each other

Share Your Day
□ Share what really went on during the day
□ Include your partner in your daily activities
□ Be interested in what he or she is interested in (as much as possible) (2)

Share Activities That Are Fun
□ Spend quality time together (2)
□ Develop mutual hobbies (3)
□ Plan vacation time together (2)
□ Spend relaxed time together (2)
□ Be spontaneous; drop everything and go away together for the weekend
□ Suggest doing new and exciting things together
□ Do activities together that are fun (2)
□ Get out of the house together sometimes
□ Take classes together
□ Go to the park and enjoy life together
□ Take time away from normal life; escape
□ Take time away from the children for a date, movie, etc.
□ Get involved together in society

Share Financial Responsibility
□ Make major purchases together
□ Go over finances together
□ Purchase things both partners need and want
□ Get a clear understanding together of incomes and expenses

Share Work Around the House
□ Divide household chores equitably (3)
□ Rotate who does what unpleasant tasks
□ Clearly establish tasks or chores
□ Take turns keeping the children
□ Share obligations like picking up children
□ Shop for groceries together

Share an Interest in Improving the Marriage
□ Attend marriage counseling together (2)

Share Responsibility
□ Don't have one person be in charge of the family; be a team

Neil Jacobson and Gayla Margolin suggest that a few days be desig-
nated "love days."[4] On those days, each partner does two special activities from the spouse's list. Still other days might be named "pamper-
your-partner days," in which one spouse lavishes attention on the other,
showering him or her with positive activities from the list.

One of our friends, Carl Miller, gave his wife a Christmas present of
fifty-two slips of paper, each with a particular surprise. Each Sunday
morning for a full year, with great ceremony, he brought a jar filled with
these slips to Debbie, who then chose one activity for the week.

An essential part of love days, caring days and pamper-your-partner
days is the partner's response. The partner must catch the spouse doing
something nice and thank him or her.

Your marriage will be enriched when you think up fresh activities to
break up the normal routines. Use creativity to make your love for your
spouse new every morning.

Anticipate Stressful Transitions

Life transitions—such as childbirth, having a child enter school, having
a child enter adolescence, having a child leave or move back·home,
changing jobs or retirement—disrupt schedules. In doing so, the life
changes throw the intimacy-distance-coaction balance out of sorts. Transitions may create thunderous tempests or may pass with hardly a breeze.

While many effects of life transitions cannot be avoided, some can be
moderated if the changes are anticipated. Certainly, when major life
events occur unexpectedly, we must deal not only with the event itself
but also with the disorientation of surprise. Books, lectures or audio-
tapes may suggest useful ways for dealing with the disruptions we might
encounter.

Many suggestions offered by my students (see table 2) advocate supporting and respecting the spouse. Support and respect are crucial during times of instability. Sacrifices are often necessary.

Balancing Schedules

Probably the best way to prevent incipient problems from growing is to change our schedules to allow for more intimacy, coaction or distance. One special problem for Christians is overinvolvement. While Christians don't have a monopoly on being overinvolved, their social conscience and the high value they place on the family make it likely that their commitments will outweigh their resources, especially during the child-rearing years.

For the overloaded parent, the trail out of the jungle of overcommitments begins with a map. The map indicates current commitments and measures them against a time budget. In the same way that finances must be budgeted, so must time. Hard choices are necessary.

Sometimes the packs must be divided differently—lightening the load on one parent while the other assumes more responsibility for child care or household duties. Other times new paths for the use of leisure hours must be blazed to allow more activities that both partners enjoy. Sometimes, the partners want to travel in different directions toward a commonly desired destination, and a compromise is necessary so they can stay on parallel tracks.

Once out of the jungle, the couple can add other activities, such as pursuing mutual hobbies, spending time with mutual friends, taking classes together or simply sharing each other's lives.

In general, partners need to compare their actual lifestyle to their desired lifestyle to discern threats to their closeness. Is one spouse a workaholic, leaving little time for activities as a family or as a couple? Is one spouse addicted to drugs or alcohol, organizing the life of the family around the addiction? Is the couple financially overcommitted so that the burden of debt mires the relationship in immobility? Are the spouses so hooked on television, reading, video games or other compulsions that there's no time to increase intimacy? Has pursuit of pleasure become a compulsion? If these lifestyles have become tyrants, it's time for a rebellion.

Emotional Distance and Isolation

Couples can become emotionally distant, growing apart over time until they feel that there is little or no connection between them. They may simply feel out of touch with each other.

At a more serious level—probably because the disengagement has persisted over time—couples might become emotionally insulated or isolated from each other. Their needs for intimacy, distance and coaction might be met or unmet, but emotionally insulated or isolated partners do not minister effectively to each other's needs. The emotional cutoff is almost intentional. Both partners may protest that they do not like emotional isolation, but whenever intimacy becomes a possibility, both resist.

The Distancer-Pursuer Pattern

An emotional distancer-pursuer pattern may develop.[5] Usually, the pursuer is an extroverted, expressive person who craves emotional stimulation. The emotional distancer is an introverted, self-controlled person who likes to keep his or her emotions on a short rein. Over time, the emotional pursuer and distancer set up a predictable pattern.

The pursuer demands more intimacy from the distancer. The tactics used are varied, but they usually include crying and complaining about rejection. The distancer feels threatened by demanded closeness and evades it by pouring himself or herself into work, intellectualizing or simply avoiding the spouse. The distancer may even express anger, which drives the emotional pursuer away. Another common tactic is for the distancer to use alcohol or drugs to excess. Becoming drunk or high distances the spouses. Also, if intimacy is achieved, the distancer can blame the alcohol or drugs.

This pattern may go on for years: the pursuer pursues, the distancer pulls away. Over time, the pursuer becomes exhausted and may finally cease pursuing. After a while, the distancer notices that the distance between the spouses is uncomfortably great, and this stimulates him or her to approach the pursuer. Usually, the pursuer will then reject the distancer, saying, "Where were you all those years when I needed your support?" Hurt, the distancer may withdraw and insulate himself or herself behind an emotional barrier from which criticisms and insults may be lobbed at the pursuer.

While the distancer-pursuer pattern is easier to deal with in the early stages, it isn't impossible to handle even in its well-developed form when it is fueled by constant criticism and mutual rejection.

The solution is simple to say, hard to carry out. Both spouses must give up what they have been saying for years and accept what is realistically possible.

The pursuer has been saying, "We never have enough intimacy. You avoid intimacy. We have to be closer to have a good marriage." In fact, it's likely that the emotional pursuer selected his or (usually) her mate with some care. The pursuer usually does not want as much intimacy as he or she claims. The felt need is heightened because of the pursuit. People want what seems to be denied them—even when they don't really want it. The emotional pursuer usually chose his or her mate *because* the mate was a distancer. Distance is maintained by demanding more intimacy than the distancer can tolerate, which predictably scares the distancer into flight.

The emotional distancer likewise usually does not want as much distance as (usually) he claims. If near-isolation was really the distancer's goal, why did this person choose a mate who would pursue? The distancer *wants* emotional contact—but only a moderate amount. Used to being hotly pursued for emotion, the distancer usually reacts to demands for closeness with knee-jerk flight.

If the pursuer and distancer can accept that they both want a moderate amount of emotional closeness, they can change their almost computer-programmed chase behavior. The emotional pursuer must stop making demands for intimacy, turning his or her attention to other aspects of the relationship, such as communication, and to building more independence from the distancer. Perhaps new activities might be undertaken, new classes attended, new friends sought.

The distancer will probably greet with relief this change in demand for emotional intimacy. There will be a respite from the demands. The pursuer's deepest fears—that the spouse has totally and permanently withdrawn from the relationship—will usually be activated. If the couple is to break their pattern, though, the emotional pursuer must not succumb to the temptation to try to pressure the spouse into more intimacy.

After a while, the distancer will be ready for more closeness. But the distancer will not be in the habit of requesting intimacy. It is usually helpful for the couple to schedule a specific time to discuss how they wish to manage their intimacy. It is essential that this time not be scheduled in the midst of an emotional crisis. Though crisis periods are to be avoided, the couple need not wait for a time of *no* stress; such a time will never come.

With stressful circumstances at a minimum, the discussion can be calm and anxieties kept at bay. Both partners will likely find this situation conducive to coming up with agreements that will suit them both.

Emotional Overinvolvement

Couples may become overinvolved with each other. This is less common than emotional distance between partners, but it still occurs, especially with couples who have not been married long or those who have been very dependent on their parents and continue that pattern into their marriages.

The overinvolved couple can rarely stand to be apart. They eat together, shower together, talk for long hours, share almost all their leisure time and appear to their friends as inseparable. The difficulty is the long-term strain that overinvolvement causes. One spouse usually feels dominated by the other, surrendering wants, wishes and dreams in return for emotional security. Occasionally, each spouse feels controlled by the other. They may harbor resentment and anger and not express it. Expressing any negative emotions would threaten their "idyllic" relationship.

Couples who argue heatedly may also be overinvolved, but they often mistake their conflict for a lack of intimacy. Usually, people think of intimacy as warmth, good feelings and approval. They fail to see that spouses locked in a head-to-head struggle may be more emotionally intertwined than apparently blissful couples.

Love's opposite is uninvolvement, not conflict. Conflictual couples are often far from uninvolved.

Yet continual conflict is not fun. Negative intimacy is costly. Given the choice, almost everyone would choose peaceful bliss over all-out war. We usually want to reduce the negative intimacy of conflict.

The most straightforward way to reduce conflict is to use some of the conflict-management strategies that will be discussed in chapter nine. But how do Beleaguered Battlers, Weary Warriors or Fearsome Fighters spend their time once they have reduced their conflict? Positive intimacy-producing activities, such as those discussed in the early parts of this chapter, must be substituted.

In counseling, my first assignment to couples in conflict is usually small. They must set aside thirty minutes each night for a week and read aloud the book *Getting to Yes: Negotiating Agreement Without Giving In,* by Roger Fisher and William Ury.[6] Not only do they learn a method of handling conflict, but they generally enjoy the time together as well.

Usually, emotionally overinvolved partners must combat two mistaken beliefs. Overinvolved partners may believe that spouses must meet all of each other's emotional needs. Actually, this is true only of sexual intimacy. It's best to find a balance between the partner and family members or friends as providers of other types of intimacy.

The second mistaken belief equates fusion and intimacy. Again, a balance is needed, this time between individualism and unity, autonomy and connectedness. Christian discipleship is built on a subtle blend of uniting with God and maintaining individual personality. Even within the Godhead, the trinity is three individuals within a unified whole. In Christianity, there is no fusion with God in which we lose our personality. The same is true in marriage.

Getting past overinvolvement can be traumatic, because the overinvolved couple's fundamental ideas about marriage will probably be challenged. They must remain assured that intimacy is valued, but they must also strive to develop independence from each other.

If you have been overinvolved with your spouse, perhaps it's time for each of you to engage in different hobbies or pastimes. Look for a few differences in likes and dislikes and in personality style. If you maintain your value on unity, your attention to differences should provide freedom rather than separation.

Creating Sexual Closeness

A final problem in closeness is sexual difficulties. A sexually troubled couple may have difficulties because one or both partners have sexual dysfunctions, or they may simply have lost the spark from their sexual relationship.

Sexual difficulties not serious enough to be labeled "problems" may still take some of the joy from the marriage relationship. Change is possible. The four-level PLISSIT model provides a good way to understand how a couple can improve their sexual relationship.[7]

The P in PLISSIT stands for *permission*. At the first level, the couple needs permission to engage in sexual behavior about which they may have some doubts. For instance, some couples pursue the mystic ideal of the simultaneous orgasm through intercourse and are dismayed when the husband ejaculates before the wife is near to orgasm. That couple needs freedom from an ideal that shackles them. The fact is that most couples have sequential orgasm. Usually, one spouse stimulates the other to orgasm, and after that the other spouse is stimulated to orgasm.

Similarly, some spouses have misconstrued married sex as a duty; consequently, they have denied themselves pleasure. These spouses need freedom from their mistaken beliefs about sexuality.

At the second level, the LI stands for *limited information*. Couples can obtain helpful information by reading books about sexuality. Some fine books by Christians discuss sexuality within the marriage.

At the third level, the SS stands for *specific suggestion*. When couples have specific concerns, they may find answers in books or by consulting trusted friends, pastors or counselors.

At the fourth level, the IT in PLISSIT stands for *intensive therapy*. Usually, marriage therapists or sex therapists are best prepared to help the couple that is experiencing sexual dysfunction.

For some couples, the bedroom is merely another arena for conflict.

Often this shows up as a sexual dysfunction in one or both partners. But sexual dysfunction is not always a sign of a power struggle within the marriage. There may be physical reasons for it. Spouses who experience such dysfunctions should be examined by a physician to determine whether there are physical causes for their problems.

If physical causes have been ruled out, the couple must decide whether to seek help from a marital therapist or sex therapist or whether they should try to work out the problems on their own. If the couple has had prolonged sexual dysfunction, I would advise them to seek professional help. Often a professional can help solve a problem quickly, while a home remedy may make the problem more intractable. With that caveat, here are some of the common treatments for sexual dysfunctions for couples who wish to try to solve such problems on their own.[8]

The most common sexual dysfunction among men is secondary impotence. Secondary impotence is inability to achieve or sustain an erection that will permit sexual intercourse. In secondary impotence, the man *develops* impotence after a period of satisfactory functioning. This is different from primary impotence, which is *never* having been able to sustain an erection.

Most men experience occasional impotence at times of stress, after drinking alcohol or during extreme tiredness. This is not considered a sexual dysfunction. But when impotence occurs most of the time (or if the man is extraordinarily bothered by occasional impotence), then it is considered to be a sexual dysfunction.

Sex therapists can successfully treat primary impotence in about 60 percent of the cases and secondary impotence in about 75 percent of the cases. Generally, to treat the problem, the husband and wife are told to engage in pleasurable sexual caresses; intercourse is prohibited during this "teasing" phase. After erection is consistently achieved, the wife sits astride the husband and inserts the penis, holding it and squeezing it with her vagina; no thrusting is permitted. The third phase involves gentle thrusting.

Premature ejaculation, which is ejaculating prior to entering the woman or shortly after entering her, is men's second most common sexual problem. It is particularly common among young men. Usually, with sexual experience, the man can learn to recognize the signs of imminent ejaculation and reduce the stimulation before ejaculation occurs.

To treat this problem, the couple arouse each other, and the wife presses hard just below the head of the penis whenever the man becomes very aroused. The pain reduces the husband's arousal. After he has regained control, the couple returns to lovemaking. The husband learns to recognize his feelings just before the onset of ejaculation so he can stop thrusting or withdraw the penis if necessary until he calms down. Usually it takes only a few sessions to deal with the problem.

When a man is capable of sexual intercourse but has little interest in it, the dysfunction is called "low sexual desire." There are two types of men with low sexual desire—those with only occasional sexual interest and those with phobic or near-phobic fear of intercourse. Low sexual desire may be caused by a low testosterone level, having been sexually abused as a child, strong fear of intimacy, or power struggles.

Low sexual desire is considered a difficult problem to treat. Treatment usually involves marital therapy along with sexual therapy. Often the different level of sexual interest between man and woman must be accepted, and the couple can work out other ways of meeting the wife's sexual needs. For example, the couple may have intercourse infrequently, and at other times the wife may be caressed to orgasm.

For women, the most frequently reported sexual dysfunctions are primary or secondary orgasmic dysfunctions. Primary orgasmic dysfunction is never having had an orgasm; secondary orgasmic dysfunction is dissatisfaction with the frequency of orgasms or the means by which they are achieved.

Primary orgasmic dysfunction is successfully treated in about five-sixths of the cases. Typically, women are taught to experience the look and feel of their own genitals and to learn about their sexual feelings and sensations. They stimulate themselves, using their hands or a vibrator (if necessary) and fantasy, until they are able to achieve orgasm alone. Their husband is then involved in the manual stimulation and perhaps fantasies until orgasm occurs.

About 75 percent of women with secondary orgasmic dysfunction are successfully treated. Usually, treatment involves marital therapy along with use of manual stimulation, as with primary orgasmic dysfunction.

Sexual fulfillment and orgasms are not the same thing. Many women rate their sex life as satisfactory without experiencing orgasms. The nature of the orgasm has been argued and debated for years. Freud suggested that the vaginal orgasm was the only legitimate one, but Masters and Johnson later claimed that there was only one type of orgasm—the clitoral orgasm, which could come about through direct manual or oral stimulation or by indirect stimulation through sexual intercourse. Since Masters and Johnson's research, scientists have found that some women describe the clitoral orgasm and the deep vaginal orgasm differently. Another area inside and on the top of the vagina, called the Graffenberg spot, can produce a different feeling at orgasm in some women.

In research, men and women have written descriptions of their orgasms. People who read the descriptions cannot differentiate between descriptions written by men and women, which suggests that subjectively men's and women's orgasms are quite similar. There is evidence, though, that stimulating more areas of a woman's body—breasts, clitoris, vagina—and even describing a sexual fantasy simultaneously results in more bodily response and thus more intense orgasms. The same is true of orgasm in men. Stimulating penis, nipples and other parts of the skin simultaneously often results in more intense orgasms than caressing a single spot.

Another dysfunction in women is vaginismus, which is painful sensations in the vaginal area during penetration. Most vaginismus involves a phobic fear of sexual intercourse. Treatment may begin by helping the woman become desensitized to her fear or by instructing her to "stay with" her fear as she proceeds through behavioral techniques of desensitization. Vaginismus is usually successfully treated through using dilators, which can be as simple as fingers of different diameters—beginning with the tip of the husband's little finger. While the husband inserts the finger in his wife's vagina, she concentrates on relaxing her vaginal muscles. In severe cases, the wife may insert her own fingers, so that she can be confident of controlling the experience of pain, before the husband is involved.

For women, low sexual desire, which has also been called frigidity, involves a reluctance to experience sexual pleasure or to engage in intercourse. The treatment usually involves sensate focus exercises.

In sensate focus, the couple undress in a place and at a time where they will not be interrupted by phone calls, children or other distractions. They spend about a half hour each giving pleasurable bodily caresses to the other. This stage is called "pleasuring." During pleasuring, neither breasts nor the genitals may be touched.

In the second stage of sensate focus, called genital pleasuring, the genitals may be caressed, but orgasm is not allowed, nor is intromission, regardless of how sexually excited one or both partners become.

The third stage of sensate focus is nondemand coitus. The woman mounts the man and inserts his erect penis into her vagina. After holding him for a time, she may squeeze him with her vaginal muscles and begin to move slowly up and down. She is not to attend to his pleasure at all, only to the sensations she has as she moves and squeezes his penis. If he becomes too stimulated, he tells her and they rest—with him inside her or outside her—until he has regained control.

When he has regained control, they continue the woman's stimulation. The sensations and interruptions may have a teasing effect that heightens her desire. She stops whenever she feels tired. At the end of the exercise, the husband is usually allowed to have an orgasm.

In the fourth stage of sensate focus, the couple stimulate each other with the intent of orgasm. Often, coitus to orgasm is preceded by other sensate focus exercises such as pleasurable genital caressing and nondemand coitus.

Much of a couple's sexual relationship depends on their general relationship. A few couples can have excellent sexual encounters even when the rest of their marriage is falling apart, and some couples have troubled sexual relationships while the remainder of their marriage is in excellent shape. But usually there is a strong connection—at least enough of a connection that the couple with bothersome sexual problems should consider marital therapy.

Summary

How you handle problems in closeness depends on how you assess the problem. If you differ in social, recreational or intellectual intimacy from your spouse, you can usually remedy the differences by adjusting your schedules to provide more time for intimacy, distance or coaction. If you differ in emotional intimacy from your spouse, you can (1) change patterns of emotional distancing or pursuing or (2) decrease over-involvement with each other. If you differ in sexual intimacy from your spouse, you can (1) feel free to experiment with new, mutually enjoyable sexual behaviors, (2) seek information about lovemaking, (3) get specific suggestions for specific sexual problems or (4) consider marital or sexual therapy for difficult sexual problems.

Closeness won't just happen. You have to work to achieve the degree of closeness that will satisfy you both.

8

Communication

When Alexander Graham Bell sent his voice through wires to the next room, it was a virtual miracle. Now, we ricochet messages off distant satellites and scoop them up halfway round the world in seconds. Yet, amid these technological marvels, people can't seem to communicate one-on-one any better than they could thousands of years ago. Information saturates our brains. We have difficulty organizing our thoughts. Life is too fast-paced, with constant demands for change. We have become adept at receiving information passively and reacting emotionally, but we are inept at transmitting information effectively.

Communication strains are often felt in our marriages. After you examine your marital communication, you can try the suggestions for change that seem appropriate to your marriage.

Assessing Your Communication Patterns

When people live together, they develop *patterns* of communication. Over time, marital communication becomes so practiced that it appears almost to be scripted. The scripts may be sound bites, brief dialogues or one-act plays.

Such patterning is useful when communication is going well. Partners more or less know what to expect as they exchange information. By following the pattern, they don't have to think about nonverbal information, context and style of delivery. They can focus on what is being communicated.

When communication isn't going well, though, the patterns can be destructive. Partners assume the worst, predicting that the spouse has negative intentions and attitudes. Poor communication perpetuates misunderstanding and traps the couple into additional negative communications in a vicious cycle.

Your first important step in evaluating your communication is to understand your general assumptions about your love for each other.

☐ List the positive aspects of your spouse's love and care for you.

☐ What assumptions do you make about his or her attempts to communicate?

☐ Do you believe that your spouse wants to have negative or positive communication?

☐ When communication goes awry, do you think it is because your spouse *wants* to misunderstand or be misunderstood, or is it because you or your spouse is somehow *unable* to communicate effectively?

At a second level, try to understand your typical communication patterns. Communications around certain topics tend to follow set pathways.

For each of the following topics, describe how communication usually takes place.

☐ 1. How is sex initiated? Who asks? How is the asking done—physical caresses or words? Is sex "spontaneous," or do you set "dates"?

☐ 2. How are important decisions made? Unimportant ones? Pick several decisions and describe how they are discussed and made. Who says what? When?

☐ 3. How are you each romantic (not in a sexual sense)? How do you know when your partner is being romantic? Perhaps neither of you is romantic, or perhaps one is but the other isn't. How is romance handled if one is romantic and the other is not?

☐ 4. How do you deal with the in-laws? How does your spouse deal with your parents? Interacting with our parents can plunge us back into adolescent ways of acting. Does either of you act markedly different when you are around your or your spouse's parents?

There are many situations in which patterns of behavior recur. Some may be important to your marriage.

☐ List situations that are unique to your marriage in which you see particularly patterned communications.

Combinations of communications at the broadest level are called *roles.* One example of husband-and-wife roles may be that the husband is the "head of the house" and his spouse is the "submissive wife." It is important to note that couples may label roles similarly but not expect similar behaviors to make up the roles. One wife said, "He is the head of the house. He makes all the important decisions in the family, such as what our positions on the budget deficit and the oil crisis are, whom to vote for in political elections and what our attitude toward Iran is. As a submissive wife, I only make the trivial decisions, such as how we spend our money, where we go on vacation and how we will raise our children."

The Bible gives the general guideline that husband and wife are both to cultivate the attitude attributed to Christ in Philippians 2:6-9: being willing to lay down their own rights for each other. Thus it's important that a couple have harmony in their roles and not make each other miserable arguing about who is correct.

☐ Describe how you each understand the husband's and the wife's roles in the marriage. Do you agree in your understanding? Are you more willing to insist that you understand roles correctly or to lay aside your understanding in love?

Assessing Your Daily Communications

While roles describe many communications generally, some communications are more momentary. Something comes up and you respond to it. Perhaps you are reading the paper and an article catches your attention. Perhaps you hear something interesting on television, you watch a movie together, or a teacher calls to talk about your son's difficulty completing his homework. These daily communications create much of the general feeling of closeness between partners.

Although some people have difficulty communicating any feelings, most people can communicate most of their feelings easily within marriage. Still, people often have difficulty communicating *certain* feelings. For example, one couple could easily communicate anger, but sadness was off-limits. Another marriage had a strong prohibition against communicating *any* negative emotion, whether it be anger, sadness or fear. The couple usually replaced those feelings with more "acceptable" ones that conveyed their discomfort—disgust, frustration, peevishness, discontent.

Objectively assess your daily communications. Consider questions such as these:

☐ 1. How often do you communicate? Are you satisfied with this frequency?

☐ 2. What is the emotional tone of the communication? Is it usually cooperative, informative, positive, negative?

☐ 3. How open is your communication? Are certain topics taboo? What can't you talk about?

☐ 4. How well do you understand each other? Do you communicate on the same "wavelength"?

☐ 5. Which feelings can you communicate easily?

☐ 6. How do you make requests of each other? Are requests clear and straightforward, or must they be made subtly or indirectly—almost under disguise? Are they made politely, or are they given as orders or in a manner that implies that one partner takes the other for granted?

Assessing Your Negative Communications
Finally, sometimes negative patterns of communication can develop within even the best marriages.

Negative communications can be grouped into five categories. In the first, called "Run Away" strategies, negative aspects of the marriage are maintained by not confronting them. "Help Your Spouse" strategies maintain a negative atmosphere by subtly blaming the spouse while ostensibly "helping." The most varied category of negative communication strategies is "Use Guilt Creatively." Making the spouse feel guilty can be done with the subtlety of a scalpel or the directness of a sledgehammer. Regardless of how guilt is produced, though, it elevates one spouse by putting down or diminishing the partner. In the "Gotcha" category, hostility becomes more observable, with a mentality of "scoring points" being foremost. Finally, in the "Give No Quarter" category, pitched war is the motif, and coercive threats of separation and divorce punctuate the couple's interactions.

Complete the "Checklist of Negative Communications" below to see whether your marriage has been invaded by any of these marauders.

Checklist of Negative Communications
Instructions: Under each heading, make a check by the negative communication strategies you can remember using within your marriage during the past year. Make an X if you remember a time within the past year that your spouse used one of these communication strategies.

Run Away
☐ Simply refuse to discuss the issue, regardless of how important.
☐ Begin to discuss important issues, then leave in the middle of the discussion (preferably storming out while angry or crying).
☐ Don't acknowledge that your marriage has any problems.

Help Your Spouse
☐ Always share your opinion, whether it is asked for or not. Give your spouse loads of unsolicited help; heaven knows he or she needs it.

☐ Play psychiatrist by speculating about your spouse's motives. Concentrate on the negative motives. If your spouse denies having those motives, accuse him or her of defensiveness.

☐ Tell your spouse what he or she is thinking and feeling. This is especially effective as a means of correction after the spouse has expressed a feeling (for example, "You don't really feel depressed; you're really angry").

Use Guilt Creatively

☐ Arrange things so they are the way you want them, which makes it difficult for the spouse to object without feeling guilty.

☐ Collect injustices. Never forget.

☐ Bring up past injustices at strategic points in arguments.

☐ Act the martyr.

☐ Use your weaknesses to produce guilt (for example, "You're making my ulcer act up again").

☐ Use your strengths to produce guilt (for example, "If you'd contribute as much to the family income as I do, then you could . . .").

☐ Never accept an apology.

☐ Point out how other married couples seem to do things better than the two of you do, and how other people's partners seem not to have your partner's faults.

☐ Watch for situations that place your partner at a disadvantage (such as forgetting an anniversary). These can be used later.

☐ Make absolute statements (such as "You *never* take me out," "You *always* forget important events," "*Everyone* makes love this way").

☐ Ponder the arguments of the day while you are making love, so that orgasm becomes unlikely.

☐ Catch your spouse using any of these negative communications, and point it out to him or her (in public, if possible).

Gotcha

☐ Use a double bind, such as "Don't let people tell you what to do," or "Honey, you've got to take control of our marriage." Double binds are challenges the partner can't win regardless of how he or she responds. If "Honey" takes control of the marriage, he does so only because he is controlled into doing so, but if "Honey" does not take control of the marriage, he has no control.

☐ Use humor to put the spouse down. Always smile when you put your spouse down, and if he or she gets hurt, then accuse him or her of being too sensitive.

☐ Retaliate. Get even.

Give No Quarter
☐ Never back down in an argument.
☐ Demand that your spouse admit guilt.
☐ Threaten or use physical force to convince (or at least punish) your spouse.
☐ Threaten separation or divorce.

The five categories are arranged roughly in order of increasing severity, so if any checks congregate in the later categories, there is cause for concern about negative communication strategies.

Completing Your Assessment

If you ask people what they think the main cause of marital problems is, most will reply, "Poor communication." Yet communication is so complex that the phrase "poor communication" probably hides more than it reveals. To understand your marriage, you must carefully consider particular areas of communication.

☐ Is communication enhanced by positive expectations about the relationship or poisoned by negative expectations?

☐ Are your communication difficulties like fighting a major war against an enemy that multiplies incessantly, or are difficulties limited in scope and topic, like a besieged band of soldiers stubbornly fighting against all odds? Or are the difficulties scattered throughout the relationship like a network of guerrilla fighters, so that uncovering one pocket of resistance does not help predict where the next will be?

☐ If there is some problem in communication, is it due more to the absence of positive communication or to the presence of negative communication?

☐ Is the problem more in what is (or is not) said, in how you say it, or in what your communication reveals about the relative power each spouse has to make decisions?

☐ Is the problem on the reflex level of knee-jerk communications, or has decision making or thoughtful discussion somehow gone haywire?

☐ Are daily communications pleasant and functional, or contentious, uninformative or boring?

☐ Are some topics or emotions off-limits?

Communication occurs without ceasing. Even trying not to communicate is communication. So understanding your communication can affect the entire marriage.

By now you have spent a good deal of time thinking about how you and your spouse communicate. Return to figure 2, at the end of chapter five, and rate your marriage's communication on the Marriage Thermometer.

Intent Versus Impact

It's important to understand that what we intend to communicate is not always what we actually communicate.

Ria and Drew had separated four times previously. Each time Ria moved out, Drew pressured her to return and she caved in. They were in their fifth separation when they came to our counseling center, the Center for Psychological Services and Development. Ria was living in an apartment about an hour from Richmond. She would come to Richmond on the weekends and on the day of their scheduled counseling session, when she and Drew would go out for dinner and talk.

Their counselor, Kathy Hsu, directed them to discuss whether they intended to get back together.

RIA: I'm really nervous about getting back together. I'm nervous because I . . . well, I guess I don't have enough information.

I don't know if I'm going to be hurt again.

DREW: I think you have enough information. I've tried to reassure you that it'll be different this time. I don't know what else I can do. You just need to decide. You'll never make a decision by holding back. You can't get any more information by holding back either. The only way to find out if you're going to get hurt is to come back.

RIA: You're right. I know you're right. (Begins to cry.) It's just . . . I'm *afraid* for us to get back together.

DREW: I want to calm your fears. (He reaches out and takes her hand.) I want you to conquer those anxieties. I know you can do it, and I want to be able to support you. Just act. That's what you have to do. Just act. I'll support you.

RIA: (Sobs loudly) I can't.

Kathy stopped the discussion to discuss how the couple was communicating.

KATHY: Ria, you seemed to be very distressed through all of this.

RIA: I don't know why. I just feel so helpless.

KATHY: When you started, you said you were anxious about getting back together because you were afraid you might get hurt again. What did you *intend* to communicate to Drew? What was the main message you wanted him to get?

RIA: Just what you said. I was afraid. I *am* afraid. I guess I wanted him to know that I have very strong mixed feelings about our getting back together. I want to, but I wonder if it's worth it.

KATHY: Drew, Ria wanted to tell you that she had mixed feelings about getting back together. Is that what came across to you?

DREW: Pretty much. I understood her to say that she really wanted to get together, but some kind of neurotic fear was holding her back and I wanted to help her get past that fear.

KATHY: But that doesn't sound exactly like what Ria tried to say. It seemed that she tried to say that her feelings are of equal

strength and that she considers each feeling equally emotional and equally reasonable.

DREW: Yeah, I can kind of see that now.

KATHY: So the *intent* of Ria's communication didn't exactly agree with
the *impact* that the communication had on you.

DREW: Right.

KATHY: Now, Drew, your first communication was to encourage Ria
and to exhort her simply to decide to return. Was that your
intent?

DREW: Yes. I wanted her to act because I knew she would stay frustrated and spin her wheels by not deciding. I wanted her to
get over her distress rather than to suffer. I love her and it
hurts me to see her suffer.

KATHY: Ria, did Drew's communication have that *impact* on you?

RIA: Well, I know he loves me. He has always said that and showed
it in his own way. But I started to feel trapped. The more he
talked, the more trapped I felt. I knew he was right, but that
didn't help me be less afraid. We've separated and come back
together before, and it's always painful. When he reached out,
I felt like the long arm of the law had clamped down on me
and I couldn't get away. It was a dismal feeling.

KATHY: So you felt trapped. Drew wanted you to feel loved and supported, but his insistence that you make a decision didn't have
the impact that he intended.

RIA: It sure didn't—just the opposite.

While Ria and Drew had serious marital problems that had brought
them to counseling, their communication was actually not too bad. Each
loved the other and tried to show love. Yet their communications were
missing the mark.

Ria and Drew had to learn to interrupt their talking more frequently
and check out whether the message they intended to get across was
actually reaching the other person. They learned to let their feelings be
their guide. As long as they felt understood by each other, they didn't

interrupt their normal conversation. But if someone began to feel negative emotions, they began to ask where communication had gone haywire.

Will and Terrie had a different communication problem. They interrupted each other so that neither had time to complete a thought before the partner was off on another problem. To solve their problem, Will and Terrie had to set appointments in which each could speak his or her mind for fifteen minutes without interruption. They agreed that even if one person couldn't think of anything to say, the spouse couldn't talk until the fifteen minutes were over.

After each had talked for fifteen minutes, they entered a second phase in which one, say Terrie, would make a statement and then say "Over," as if they were talking on a CB radio. Once Terrie relinquished the floor, Will had to summarize what Terrie said before he could make his point.

Will and Terrie succeeded at this structured form of communication primarily because their communication was not marred by extreme conflict (which often impels people to violate the rules). In addition, they wanted to improve their relationship, even if it meant they felt a little silly doing it.

Changing communication patterns is not easy. There are formidable obstacles to change, such as our unwillingness to act differently, fear of the unknown if we try to change, and risk of failure or rejection.

But look who's on your side. First, your spouse is on your side. That may not always seem to be the case, but it's true. Your spouse wants a happy marriage as much as you do, so he or she will be cheering you on as you try to communicate.

Even more important, Jesus is pro-marriage. He wants you to communicate well and to build each other up. If you are determined to take the risk of bettering your communication, Jesus will help you.

Changing Communication: Listen

Conversation is always a surprise. As I sit in my living room and listen to the flow of conversation among friends, it always amazes me that conversation travels in so many unanticipated directions. Like a boxer, bobbing, ducking, weaving, vibrant conversation is unpredictable. Its unpredictability makes it exciting—and difficult.

One thing that makes conversation difficult is that we're usually at least as interested in what we are going to say next as we are in what the other person is saying now. We listen faster than other people talk, maybe as much as seven times as fast. So we tune in to the beginning of a sentence, check out, listen to the background music, watch the sun go down, wonder about whether we ate so much that we will have a sour stomach in the morning, tune back in to catch the middle of a sentence ("Yep, that's what I thought she was saying"), wonder whether the kids are still awake, have a brief association to a thought just mentioned and check the end of the sentence ("Sure enough, still headed in the same direction as the beginning of the sentence"). Our minds are so fast, it's no wonder we have trouble listening accurately.

Besides this, our ego insists that what we have to say is undoubtedly more important than what anyone else has to say. So our spare mental energy is shunted into rehearsing what we intend to say next.

One key, then, to enriching already good communication is to focus more attention on listening to our partner.

Other excellent suggestions were made by my class in effective behavior (see "Keeping It Fresh" in the previous chapter). I've summarized their suggestions in table 3, under general headings.

The first category of suggestions is simply to take time to talk together. With today's frantic pace, finding the time to spend with your spouse in a heart-to-heart can be a major trick. Sometimes Kirby and I set appointments to talk. We also periodically walk laps around the block. There is a rut in the street from our repeated circuits. Still, there never seems to be enough time to talk all we want. Pressures from work and family intrude, and often it is the momentary crisis that impels action.

Another wise suggestion is to express love and affection for your partner. It's not enough to *feel* love. *Show* it! And this is important: show love in ways that your partner wants it shown. Usually we're eager to show love in ways that *we* want it shown to us, which may not always fit with the partner's expectations.

Table 3. Suggestions for improving communication in marriage.

Communicate

Talk Together
- ☐ Take time to sit and talk
- ☐ Jointly discuss things that concern both of you
- ☐ Talk about work and friends with each other
- ☐ Set aside a time each month for special talking and discussion of problems

Express Love for Partner
- ☐ Tell the partner you love him or her at least once a day (3)
- ☐ Show affection if one or both of you like it
- ☐ Let him or her know you care

Express Admiration for Partner
- ☐ Compliment each other (4)
- ☐ Praise each other for accomplishments

Understand and Accept Spouse
- ☐ Understand your spouse (5)
- ☐ Be patient, kind and understanding
- ☐ Listen to your spouse's problems
- ☐ See things from each other's point of view
- ☐ Have spouses repeat or summarize what was just said

Accept Spouse
- ☐ Accept your spouse as he or she is (2)
- ☐ Listen when you feel attacked; don't jump to conclusions
- ☐ Never try to change your spouse

Let Your Spouse Understand You
- ☐ Tell your spouse about yourself (wishes, dreams, etc.)
- ☐ Tell your spouse what bothers you

Communicate Your Feelings
- ☐ Express your feelings honestly with sensitivity (5)
- ☐ Be honest about your feelings, but be gentle revealing things you don't like (3)
- ☐ Be truthful except when she asks, "How do I look?"—then always say "Great," whether she does or not
- ☐ Be open (2)
- ☐ Don't keep secrets
- ☐ Some secrets are best not revealed
- ☐ Be willing to communicate

□ Talk about personal feelings and views

Resolve Disagreements Peaceably
□ Be willing to compromise
□ Don't blame your spouse
□ Avoid arguments over money
□ Don't let problems build up; discuss them immediately
□ Don't argue in front of the children
□ Don't yell during disagreements
□ Talk things out rationally
□ Establish and use rules for arguing
□ Don't have children until you are both ready (2)
□ Never go to bed angry
□ Think about what you are arguing about and why

Shannon grew up in a home where love was shown through always remembering and celebrating each little triumph of life. She couldn't understand why Thomas continually forgot not only unimportant victories but also important dates like anniversaries, Mother's Day and Valentine's Day. Her husband, of course, grew up in a home where holidays were ho-hum. After he turned twelve, it had been rare even to receive a birthday present. Even when Shannon told Thomas how much little celebrations meant to her, he still forgot, and her fears that he didn't love her grew.

Express admiration for your partner. While most couples at least occasionally tell each other "I love you," fewer express frank admiration for the partner. Yet such an expression can almost transform a relationship. If each spouse genuinely admires the other, the relationship is placed on a firm footing as love between equals, which calms doubts about whether one spouse is more dependent on the other.

Understand and accept your spouse. One part of improving a good marriage that was recognized and mentioned by most people in my class is the need to clearly understand one's spouse and, even knowing all the imperfections, to accept one's spouse unreservedly.

Disclose Your Inner Self
Besides assuring your spouse that you listen to, understand and admire

him or her, allow your spouse to understand you.

Jonah was a private man. Although Suzanne knew before she married him that he was quiet, she underestimated the extent of his reserve. As the years of their marriage passed, Suzanne became more frustrated at her inability to draw Jonah out. In desperation, she initiated an affair. "I knew it was wrong," she said. "I even knew that I had lots of other ways to get the intimacy I wanted. But I was angry at Jonah, and deep down, I guess I wanted to punish him."

As the affair drew on, Jonah became aware of it, but the rejection he felt from Suzanne made him withdraw even more. He felt caught in a whirlpool that was sucking him and his marriage down.

Determined, Jonah began to talk with Suzanne about himself, his fears that their marriage would fail and the background that had led him to be so withdrawn. The couple began to attend counseling with their pastor, and Suzanne broke off the affair. After several weeks of counseling, she readily confessed it as sin.

Jonah will probably never be comfortable with disclosing his feelings, hopes, fears and dreams, but he found that he had to take the plunge for his marriage to remain alive.

Share Ideas

It's important to share ideas that excite you. Many couples grow apart because they fail to stay intellectually connected with each other. As the early years of marriage pass, partners tend to move into different worlds. Perhaps they both work. Each day they deal with different problems that force them to think creatively. Usually, they are eager to share those creative endeavors with coworkers, but too often they think that the spouse would be uninterested because he or she is not professionally employed in that area.

When I was in the navy, I taught nuclear physics at Naval Nuclear Power School in California. Kirby and I loved to spend our weekends hiking and backpacking. (That was obviously before the knees gave way, the back went out and even the pack gave up the ghost.) Reminiscing recently, Kirby began to talk about "alpha tunneling," describing how alpha particles radioactively decay. I hadn't thought about alpha tunneling for almost twenty years, but it came back with a rush—as a remembered good dream, not a nightmare. I recalled with great fondness the hike up that misty mountain in Yellowstone National Park during which I explained alpha tunneling to Kirby—who listened and remembered. That wins my prize for wifely understanding.

Now we are much more likely to talk about parenting adolescents, teen pregnancy, Christian books or even proper diet. But even when I was involved in a field as specialized as nuclear physics, we still shared intellectually.

Changing Negative Communications

Changing negative communications involves three steps: deciding to handle strong emotions differently, cultivating the use of humor and resolving to communicate more positively.

Handling Strong Feelings

Though some of us prefer to deny "negative emotions," we all feel them at times. Fear hovers over us, occupying our minds and taking away our breath. Anger stomps up to us and squeezes our guts, making us want to hit something and scream. Frustration seethes inside us, filling us to the bursting point. What do we do with those strong feelings?

Larry Crabb identifies three responses to strong feelings.[1] We may stuff them inside and bear them in stoic martyrdom, dump them on the nearest receptacle—the dog, a coworker, the children or too often our spouse—or deal with the feelings.

Freud suggested that stuffing feelings was the most harmful response. According to Freud's theory, the feelings *would* pop out, usually at the most inopportune time, in ways that we might hate later. This theory has largely been discredited, but stuffing feelings still has its costs. If we keep strong feelings down for long, we may be affected by illness—heart disease, ulcers and perhaps even cancer. Besides, it's no fun to suffer alone. An old Chinese proverb says, "Even a piece of paper is lighter if two people pick it up."

But dumping feelings is no way to share them. If we release our anger recklessly, it will have harmful effects. Vented on friends and family members, anger boomerangs. Fear spreads like a viral infection. Dumped anger may provoke strong feelings in others, and then we will have to deal with those feelings in addition to our own.

In any case, expressing strong feelings doesn't really get rid of the feelings. In fact, according to psychologist Carol Tavris, who reviewed years of research on anger, expressing strong feelings multiplies them.[2] Hitting a pillow in anger makes us madder. Yelling in rage makes us more furious.

How then do you deal productively with negative emotions? First, talk about them. Labeling our emotions provides a sense of control and confidence that empowers us to march forward. Second, try to solve the source of the problem. If the problem is interpersonal, try to change your own behavior, not the other person's. Third, accept that you may not be able to solve the problem completely. Accepting the things over which we have no control helps us control our emotions.

Larry Crabb gives five guidelines for dealing with anger within marriage.[3]

1. Be slow to anger.

2. Acknowledge when you feel angry.

3. Think through your goals, and determine which of them are blocked by your spouse's behavior; seek to meet your spouse's needs.

4. Assume responsibility for the goal of ministering to your spouse.

5. Express negative feelings if doing so serves a good purpose.

Develop Humor

Lighten up. Norman Cousins, author and professor on the medical faculty at UCLA, attributed his recovery from a serious disease to laughter.[4] Negative emotions, like depression, can reduce the effectiveness of the body's immune system and retard healing. Cousins fed himself a constant dose of humorous films, jokes and pleasant experiences during his convalescence from an illness that should have been fatal.

If laughter can have such a salutary effect in the human body, then we should expect it to benefit relationships even more. Humor depends on surprise, creativity and freshness. It turns our thinking around and renews us. These are the very elements necessary to enrich an already healthy marriage.

How do you bring more humor into your life? Most of us aren't comedians and don't want to be.

Actually, it's enough just to appreciate humor. In our family, meals are usually pleasant times of banter, telling jokes and sharing humorous anecdotes. Jonathan may share a joke he heard at school. Christen may tell a funny story. I may read a joke from *Reader's Digest.* Kirby may break out each of the children's baby books, in which we've recorded funny happenings, and read some of their favorites. Becca may make amusing comments, and Katy Anna, only seven, may entertain us with an imitation of a pop singer.

Or perhaps we'll spend much of the meal thinking of "Tom Swifties." These are one-line puns based on the Tom Swift novels, in which the author used adjectives and adverbs freely.

" 'I'm sick of illness,' the doctor said patiently," one of us may say.

" 'Do you get the point?' the nurse injected," someone else may insert sharply.

" 'I like strawberry shortcake,' the girl said strawberrily," Katy Anna may add . . . sweetly. (The idea of a pun isn't well developed in seven-year-olds, but her participation still elicits guffaws.) These efforts at humor, even though feeble at times, keep our family and marriage relationships happy and positive.

Communicating Positively

Suppose you've decided to communicate differently. Now what do you do?

First, identify the difficulty. In what kinds of communication do you fall down? Is it the ritual how-do-you-do's or common courtesies? Is it in passing along important information about your life, your work, your children? Is it sensitivity to feelings and important issues? Is it self-disclosure? Or is it discussing your marital communication when that appears called for? Do you make errors of omission—simply failing to talk enough in particular areas? Or are you talking too much?

One couple I counseled had a serious problem with self-disclosure. Both were hesitant to share thoughts and feelings. After ten sessions of counseling, they had begun to self-disclose pleasantly. That was helpful. However, then the man began to talk a good deal about his past, describing sexual adventures with past girlfriends. As you can imagine, soon the marriage was in trouble again. Now the partners were talking too much.

Second, when you decide to communicate differently, don't try to change everything at once. Large changes, especially if your partner is not aware of and in agreement with what you are trying to accomplish, can be disastrous. It is better to make small changes and progress a step at a time.

Third, begin with positive reminiscences—times when the relationship was going well. Try to reexperience the feelings in those days. How did you communicate then? Determine what parts of your communication are worth trying to recapture. Then, try to bring the positive back into your life.

Fourth, analyze situations carefully. You may get into a bad mood because of disappointments and defeats experienced outside of the home. When a gripe about your spouse surfaces, then, ask yourself, Is the gripe legitimate, or is it a product of a disappointment elsewhere? Is it important, or is it not really worth discussing? Is it a chance to blow off steam, or is it an issue that needs discussion?

If the problem is worth discussing, warn your spouse of the outside pressures before you begin to get into the issue that bothers you. For example, you might say, "Look, honey, I have a problem. A lot happened today. I broke a filling in my tooth, the dog just bit a lawyer's son, and my boss yelled at me, so I'm in a rotten mood. But I feel like we have to discuss something . . ."

Fifth, don't get so involved in the issues that you lose sight of your goal—communicating with your spouse in a positive way.

Sixth, if other attempts to change your communication fail, get a structured book on improving marriage communication, such as *A Couple's Guide to Communication,* by John Gottman and colleagues (it can be ordered from Research Press, 2612 N. Mattis Avenue, Champaign, Ill. 61820).

Finally, if all else fails, consider seeking marriage counseling to build better communication.

Summary

Everyone falls into habits of communication. When these habits make you and your partner unhappy, much work will be needed to change them. Striving to value your spouse in every communication and to avoid devaluing your spouse, you systematically change hurtful communication patterns. Listen carefully to your partner without defensiveness and without continually preparing counterarguments. Disclose your inner self, being careful to make sure you are having the effect you intend. Be willing to lay down your life for your partner. That will help you handle strong feelings in a loving way.

Rebuilding a positive environment after it has become negative is difficult. It requires love, self-sacrifice, forgiveness and closeness. Progress may well come in fits and starts, but persevere. The reward of good communication is life and joy.

9

Resolving Conflict

Marriage is one long conversation,
chequered by disputes.
ROBERT LOUIS STEVENSON

Marriage resembles a pair of shears,
so joined that they cannot be separated;
often moving in opposite directions,
yet always punishing anyone who comes between them.
SYDNEY SMITH

Like a bridge over troubled waters, I will lay me down.
PAUL SIMON AND ART GARFUNKEL

Conflict in marriage is not only inevitable but necessary. Husband and wife, reared in different families, have learned from their upbringing how marriages should and shouldn't operate. As their marriage begins, the relationship diverges from the individual components from which it was made. For marriage is more than parental history, more than the sum of individual experiences. Each marriage has its own identity.

This identity doesn't just happen. It is born as partners rub their sharp edges against each other, either breaking off jagged hunks that prod and stick the spouse or polishing each other into smoothly meshing cogs. The teeth of this marriage grinder are the multitude of conflicts that a couple must resolve.

Conflict is not necessarily emotional, does not necessarily involve argument and may not even be noticeable to the participants. Conflict happens as partners work together to resolve differences and find mutually satisfying solutions.

Persuasion marks the initial step in conflict resolution. Each spouse states his or her desires and tries to persuade the partner to agree. Persuasion may involve a variety of verbal strategies, including logic, and nonverbal strategies, such as becoming tearful or even depressed.

Power-sharing tension may occur over who has the ability to define a relationship. Every time a decision is made, power is shared, either equally or unequally. Couples usually arrive at some balanced distribution of power, but in some cases, power becomes distributed unequally, and partners become locked in a struggle over how the relationship will be defined.

Power strategies are attempts to relieve the power-sharing tension when a couple is at odds on who has the power to make certain decisions. Power strategies may be played to win or, just as likely, to spoil the winner's victory.

Once couples become stuck, using power strategies habitually, each partner usually attributes their "stuckness" to the other's personality. They may wail, "He's so stubborn," or "She's such a nag."

The conflicted couple, over time, develops a habit of resisting each other's attempts to resolve differences. At first, both spouses try persuasion. If that doesn't work, they experience power-sharing tension. Finally, they become locked in a power struggle, and each draws the obvious conclusion: the problem must lie in my spouse's personality.

Where does the problem lie? What is the root of the conflict? Although poor persuasive efforts, power strategies and unyielding personalities all play a part in perpetual conflict, the root cause of conflict is disagreement over who has the power to make decisions in the marriage.

Topics of Conflict

Chances are, if you have conflict with your spouse, you feel that you are simply discussing *the issues.* The issues could be virtually anything, but couples commonly argue about sex, affection, money, child rearing or discipline, in-laws, household responsibilities, use of leisure time and style of communication.

Arguments are not fun. When you are involved in an argument, you want to arrive at a solution—quickly. Therefore, it seems that the most important part of conflict is reaching agreement. For the counselor, though, the *topic* of disagreement is less important than the *method* by which the couple tries to reach agreement. Counselors find that couples who solve one disagreement will usually have another, another and another. A couple in frequent conflict can reduce conflict *not* by resolving each argument but by finding a *method* of resolving arguments effectively.

Assessing Your Conflicts

Learning *how* to resolve conflicts will involve practicing six skills:

☐ listen to, understand and communicate respect for and valuing of your spouse,

☐ observe your individual style of conflict and how it meshes with your spouse's style,

☐ perhaps most important, give up the fundamental struggle over who has the power to make decisions,

☐ stop arguments when they have become unproductive,

☐ practice solving problems without getting sidetracked,

☐ learn how to negotiate agreement without either of you having to give up things that are important to you.

Assess your usual practice in each of the preceding six areas. Let's look in more detail at each of these areas.

Understanding

☐ How well and how consistently do you listen to, understand, value and communicate respect for your spouse *during the heat of disagreement?*

You make a statement, and your spouse disagrees. You are dumb-founded. How can he or she not agree? You try to explain— rationally and calmly. Your spouse does likewise, apparently not understanding your position. You explain again, this time more loudly and with more feeling. Adrenaline rises, and pressure builds behind the eyes. It feels as if a mighty river is rushing in your ears. You grit your teeth and make a silent pact to give it one more try. Maybe if you speak slowly in words of one syllable, your spouse will grasp your point. If not . . .

In times of disagreement, the overriding focus of attention is on *being understood*. Our ideas make sense to us, and we believe that once our spouse understands our reasoning, reason will prevail. It's not natural to focus on understanding our spouse. Our brains are organized to confirm what we already believe, not to open up nondefensively to other ideas. Too often, we succumb to the natural.

Good communication, though, depends more on understanding than on being understood. If we understand our spouse and communicate that to him or her, we will often reap similar understanding.

Communicating understanding involves active listening, in which you accurately summarize what your spouse says, thinks, feels, wants and needs. Your spouse's feelings about the issue are usually as important as the meaning he or she is trying to communicate.

☐ How hard do you try to show your spouse that you understand him or her when you are in the midst of a disagreement, and how much do you try to get him or her to understand you?

☐ Could you do more to show your spouse that you understand him or her?

☐ Do you listen well, or do you need to improve your listening?

☐ Do you communicate your appreciation for and respect of your spouse, especially nonverbally, while you are disagreeing and imme-diately after? Do you tell your spouse *in words* that you love, respect and admire him or her?

By answering these questions, you can gauge how hard you try to understand your spouse, which is crucial to breaking up harmful conflict patterns and building new ones.

Style of Conflict

☐ Observe your individual style of conflict and how it meshes with your spouse's.

Richard is thoroughly logical and unemotional. His life is dedicated to rational thinking. When he disagrees with someone, he pulls into his own mind, marshals his arguments until he has thought out a good case and then presents the arguments forcefully, with evidence supporting each point.

Sybil is spontaneous and emotional. She loves to *talk* things out rather than *think* things out. After a conversation that ranges widely over the issues, she can usually arrive at a good understanding and take a productive stand on what she should do.

Together, these two are dynamite. When a difference of opinion arises, Richard tries to pull into himself, and Sybil tries to draw him into a conversation. He tries to keep control over his emotions, while she lets her emotions have full expression, saying that feelings are important data for decision making. Richard stresses principled decision making, and Sybil stresses what she wants to do. It looks as if they are ready for Judge Wapner's court.

Yet Richard and Sybil have been married for twenty-seven happy years. They have had their share of disagreements as they have reared two children through college. Still, through it all, they have been able to resolve conflicts productively. How?

In their rocky first year of marriage, they almost separated over their different styles of conflict. But they used the adversity to learn about each other's style, and they used this knowledge to manage many later conflicts.

When a disagreement crops up, Sybil knows that Richard will not want to talk about it, so she doesn't demand that he explain his reasoning early in their discussions. Richard knows that he cannot simply hole up as he works out a carefully reasoned approach to their conflict, so he tries to listen to Sybil and help her talk her way through some of the issues. Usually, Sybil will emerge from their conversation with some sense of what she thinks should be done, and she feels ready to take action. But she avoids trying to stampede Richard into a decision; she lets him take time to study.

Being very contemplative, Richard would take several months to solve most problems if he had his way. So several days after the initial discussion, Sybil asks Richard about his thinking concerning their disagreement. If he feels ready to discuss the issue, they do, because Sybil always seems ready to talk. If Richard is not yet ready to discuss, he asks for more time.

If you asked Richard and Sybil to describe how they resolve their differences, they probably could not identify this pattern. For them, the pattern simply grew like a phoenix out of the ashes of their first disastrous year of marriage.

Richard and Sybil's styles of conflict are about as opposite as possible, but they have worked out a way of conflict resolution that works for them, even though it might be a terrible way for other couples to solve problems.

Donald and Charlene also have different problem-solving styles. Donald simply doesn't like conflict and hates to talk about it. Charlene is a middle-school counselor who has been trained to value communication and regularly practices conflictual communication in her job. Again, at first blush, Donald and Charlene don't look as if they have a great future as a couple. Yet over time, they have developed a problem-solving strategy that works for them.

When a disagreement arises between Charlene and Donald, she asks him what he wants to do. If he has strong feelings, he usually says so. If he is less invested in the outcome, Charlene has implicit approval to discuss the conflict with a friend. She and her friend explore the pros and cons until she arrives at a solution to the problems. She then comes back to Donald and discusses *both sides of the issue* until they arrive at a mutual decision.

Donald and Charlene's method of solving their problems makes some people wince. It goes against most of what theorists think good communication *should* be. Intimate family secrets are shared with people outside the family. Donald is allowed to avoid communication. Yet the process works for Donald and Charlene, and I think that is *good* conflict management. Neither person feels unfairly used, and both feel that the decisions are equitable. This problem-solving method works with Donald and Charlene because there is a special trust between them.

Charlene says, "Donald knows that I always support him when I discuss issues with one of my girlfriends. I never put him down, and he knows that I never share extremely personal conflicts—such as if we were to have a conflict over our sex life. We each discuss our positions in our own way. Donald is more the 'bottomline' type of guy, the president type. I'm more the staff person who can understand and present reasoning on all sides."

Donald chimes in, "This is just our individuality. Sure, I know we're not like some other couples, but we love each other and we both know it. Charlene knows that if I really feel strongly about something, I'll tell her. She usually honors that."

I am not recommending either of these couples' problem-solving styles for anyone else. I am simply pointing out that even if spouses have widely divergent styles of conflict resolution, they can still live together in harmony by understanding and using their differences.

Your first step, then, is understanding your conflict style and determining how it meshes or clashes with your partner's.

Power Struggles

☐ Do you have power struggles in your marriage?

Marriage is two people becoming one flesh. They must work together, like the muscles in an arm or a leg. If the leg is working properly, muscles in the powerful quadriceps on top of the thigh contract and the hamstring muscle on the back of the thigh extends in coordinated harmony. Then hamstrings contract and quadriceps extend. The person is propelled along in a smooth gait. However, if the muscles try to contract simultaneously, the result is paralysis. The muscles lock up, a muscle spasm begins and pain follows.

In the "one flesh" of marriage, a power struggle is like a muscle spasm. Two muscles that are designed to work in harmony try to act in opposition. The marriage is paralyzed, with the couple being unable to make decisions and resolve differences. Pain begins.

A power struggle is a fundamental disagreement over who can say what will occur and how decisions are made, not over what the decision actually is.[1]

Consider a marriage in which most decision making is shared. If the wife announces that she is going back to work one month after the birth of a child, a power struggle may well follow even if the husband agrees with her decision. He is upset because she made the decision unilaterally.

Power struggles are easy to detect. If, after a discussion, you find yourself having imagined conversations with the other person, mentally rehearsing your next conversation, feeling that your basic rights have been violated, then you are probably in a power struggle. Such mental dialogues might sound like this. "Who does she think she is, telling me that she's going back to work? That's going to affect me as much as her. She doesn't run my life. We're supposed to be a partnership. She doesn't have the *right* to just give me an order." The mental conversation may continue as the aggrieved spouse rehearses the things he intends to say to his spouse the next time. These may include biblical verses about "headship," concerns about the baby's intellectual, emotional and spiritual development, explanations about how the unilateral decision is inconsiderate, or other reasons why the decision should be reconsidered.

In this emotional issue, the point is easy to miss: The couple is in a *power struggle*. The husband is offended not because the wife made a mistake (in his opinion), but because she violated the implicit rules about how decisions are to be made.

A power struggle may occur anytime existing decision rules are violated. Susan and Judd shared decision making according to their areas of expertise. Susan, a businesswoman, kept account of the finances. Judd, an artist, cared for the yard and interior of the house. But after Susan read a book about "Christian marriage," which described traditional husband-wife roles as the biblical plan for marriage, she announced that Judd should take over the management of family finances.

While Judd was flattered that Susan wanted him to be in control, he felt uneasy and didn't know why. He was uneasy because in reality *Susan* had assumed control of the family by announcing that Judd should have control. The issue was not *who* was to "head" the family. The issue was *who had the power to say* who was to "head" the family.

Power struggles are generally at the heart of persistent marital conflict. At the core of power struggles are selfishness and lack of consideration.

☐ Survey your marriage for the presence of power struggles. In general, who has the power to make decisions?

Probably you'll find that power to make decisions is determined differently for different areas. In some cases, the husband will have most of the authority; in others, the wife will decide. In many areas, the decision-making authority will be shared or alternated.

☐ List the topics about which frequent disagreements occur—sex and affection, money, child rearing or discipline, household responsibilities, in-laws, use of leisure time, style of communication—and other topics that you know are issues in your marriage. Assess how you make decisions in each area. Note any areas that involve frequent power struggles.

Style of Solving Problems
☐ What happens when you have a disagreement? Do you get into unproductive arguments? If so, can the two of you stop the argument and get on to more productive problem-solving negotiations?

Stopping unproductive arguments is important to prevent negative feelings from building up and hurtful words from being exchanged. One way to stop an argument is for one spouse simply to refuse to argue or to walk out. This usually isn't a good strategy. As you now know, when one person terminates an argument unilaterally, a power struggle will be created or intensified. The spouse will think, "How dare he just walk away? Who does he think he is?" or "She doesn't have the *right* to. . ." Such thoughts are sure indicators of a power struggle. If a power struggle was already going on, after one spouse ends the argument by walking away there will be two power struggles to resolve.

Other skills related to controlling oneself during arguments involve *leveling* and *editing*.[2] Leveling is telling the spouse what you really think, feel, want and need. Many relationships are troubled because spouses do not level with each other. Most of the time, Doris harbors her feelings and expects Jim-Bob to read her mind. When he fails to guess what she wants, she accuses him of not loving her. She needs to learn how to level with Jim-Bob.

But leveling can be taken too far. Jim-Bob levels with Doris, and it causes problems. He frequently tells her what he thinks of her, feels about her and needs from her when they are with other couples, just as she is leaving for work in the morning, and without regard for her feelings. He must learn to level in the proper place, time and manner.

In the midst of an argument, Jim-Bob and Doris are both ever ready to level with each other. They say whatever enters their minds. They need to learn to *edit*, to eliminate hurtful comments—threats, put-downs, name calling and insults—from their conversations.

Getting Sidetracked
☐ Determine how you get sidetracked when trying to resolve differences.

There are many ways couples can get sidetracked during problem-solving efforts. One common way is to stagnate in the problem-identification phase. Couples may do this by *cross complaining*.[3] Here is an example of cross complaining.

DORIS: You never pick up your clothes. You just walk in and drop your work clothes wherever you happen to be when you pull them off.

JIM-BOB: You're one to talk. I can't even get into the bathroom sometimes because of all the laundry hung over everything. I have to sneak out in the backyard after dark to go to the bathroom.

DORIS: That's about what I would expect of you. Your manners around the house are not good, and when company comes over, I'm always embarrassed.

JIM-BOB: *You're* embarrassed. This house is a wreck . . .

Neither Doris nor Jim-Bob responds to the other's complaint. Each merely offers another complaint.

Couples also get off-track through *metacommunicating,* which means talking about how they are communicating. Metacommunication is sometimes helpful. When communication is not working, the couple needs to talk about their communication. In that case, metacommunication is *the* issue, and only the couple's communication should be discussed. Metacommunication causes problems, though, when couples use it to avoid dealing with a problem. For example:

DORIS: Hey, let's go out to eat tonight.

JIM-BOB: Sure. How 'bout Bill's Bar-B-Q? They have a special on ribs.

DORIS: I want to go to the Rathskellar. The candlelight dinner for two is only $14.95.

JIM-BOB: Look, Doris, we just went to that namby-pamby restaurant last week. I want some *real* food.

DORIS: Don't use that tone of voice with me. You can't order me around like some macho Rambo.

JIM-BOB: What's wrong with my tone of voice? This is my house and I'll talk any way I want in here.

DORIS: You sound like a eight-year-old. (mimicking) "If I can't get my way, I'll take my ball and go home."

In this brief exchange, Doris and Jim-Bob are metacommunicating harmfully. They have gotten sidetracked from the issue of where they are going to eat tonight. (They will probably end up at Colonel Turkey-plucker's Fish and Grits Shop.) Metacommunication has gotten in the way of effective problem-solving.

Another sidetracking strategy is *insulting* the spouse. The variety of ways to insult are limitless. Some people are masters at insulting indirectly. They might use humor, tone of voice, a disdainful curl of the lip or implications that the spouse is somehow inadequate to the situation. Other people are more direct. They call names, put down the spouse or assassinate the spouse's character.

Insults sidetrack by provoking the spouse to defend himself or herself. (This defensiveness can then be discussed at length too—an extra benefit to keeping each other sidetracked.)

☐ Determine how often you get sidetracked during disagreements by cross complaining, metacommunicating or insulting.

Resolving Disagreements

☐ Determine whether you and your spouse can negotiate agreement without either feeling that he or she is always giving in.

In many conflictual situations, someone may feel that he or she must give in. Sometimes both people feel they must compromise so much that the result is unsatisfactory. In healthy marriages, both spouses are willing to give in, but usually neither partner feels that the giving in is one-sided.

☐ Assess your most recent disagreements. Was there a time when both people aired their gripes?

☐ Was this followed by some consensus about the nature of the problems that needed to be addressed?

☐ Did the first two phases of problem solving take place relatively quickly, or did the gripes and problem-definition phase take a long time?

☐ Was most of the time spent discussing potential solutions?

☐ Was a decision made?

When one spouse complains of a problem, that may be a cue for problem solving. This is especially true if the complaint is shared by the other spouse. However, the fact that someone complains does not mean that the person wants a problem to be solved. He or she may really want support rather than solution. In that case, listening and caring are all that is needed.

The first step in problem solving, then, is to determine whether there is actually a problem to solve. But even if problem solving is called for, listening and supporting are necessary. Marriage researcher John Gottman has found that men are often oriented toward problem solving, while women are more often support-oriented.[4] Whether or not that's the case in your marriage, jumping into problem solving too early can block solution of the problem.

☐ Assess whether one or both partners are prone to jump into problem-solving efforts before showing a clear understanding of what the spouse is thinking, feeling, wanting and needing.

Probably the greatest hindrance to effective conflict resolution is a couple's inability to agree on the definition of the problem to be solved. Each may see the problem from his or her own point of view, so there are actually two separate problems needing solution.

Lengthy discussions about which problem is the *real* problem indicate that a power struggle is in progress. The issue in this situation is *who can say* what the real problem is. Rather than discuss at length which problem is the real one, the couple should quickly move away from problem definition and work toward solving first one problem, then the other.

☐ For the two most recent disagreements that you can remember, did problem definition take longer than five minutes?

When solutions to a difference of opinion are proposed, they may be accepted totally, accepted partially or rejected. If the partners agree on the definition of the problem but cannot arrive at a solution, usually one or both partners are using an unproductive conflict-management strategy.

One strategy might be "yes, but."[5] In the "yes but" game, one partner proposes a solution, which the other partner rejects, giving a good reason. When this pattern happens many times, the spouse proposing solutions may become angry and accuse the yes-butter of not wanting to solve the problem.

The yes-butter becomes hurt, which makes the angry spouse sorry for his or her impatience. The angry spouse then controls his or her temper and offers more solutions. These are rejected: "Yes, but . . ." The cycle continues; it may go on and on.

While it may seem that the failure to resolve the conflict lies mainly with the yes-butter, both partners are colluding to not solve the problem. They must change this pattern if the problem is to be solved.

Another snag in problem solving is countering one solution with another. One person offers a compromise; the other person offers a second compromise. When this pattern characterizes a couple, the partners are usually involved in a power struggle. Solving the problem is less important to the couple than *who can say* what the compromise is.

A third difficulty in resolving differences is inability to arrive at good suggestions for solving the problem. This usually means that the problem has not been properly defined.

☐ In the two most recent disagreements that you remember, determine whether there is a pattern of

☐ yes but,

☐ proposing countercompromises or

☐ inability for either spouse to suggest a good solution.

You have now thought about how you and your spouse resolve your differences and handle conflict. Turn back to figure 2 (in chapter five) and use the Marriage Thermometer to rate conflict resolution in your marriage.

Learning Flexibility

Fruitful conflict resolution in marriage involves constantly adjusting the balance of power so skillfully that the couple is not even aware that there is a balance of power. While some couples seem to have explicit rules that govern how they make decisions, most have simply evolved decision-making methods.

Good marriages are usually characterized by flexible decision making. For example, spouses may have different topics in which they are expert. In the "traditional" marriage, the husband may be the expert in finances and the wife in child care. However, marriages work best when partners use their own strengths in decision making rather than rely on a formula—whether "traditional" or "egalitarian."

While the healthy marriage uses flexible decision making, it is not marked by chaos. If there are no patterns for decision making, the couple has conflict each time they make a decision. Thus, a couple needs stability in decision making but must be flexible enough to change their patterns as they encounter new circumstances.

Easing Strains

Sometimes, spouses feel perpetually uneasy and strained. They haven't located the sources of tension and conflict. Robert Liberman and his colleagues have developed a way to help couples detect points of marital strain.[6]

Write down eight potential problem areas: sex, communication, child rearing, money, leisure and social activities, household responsibilities, job, and independence-dependence. In each area, each partner writes a brief description of his or her fantasy of the ideal marriage. The ideal need not be realistic. Each partner may pick one fantasy to share with the spouse. Together, they then try to agree on some steps that would approach that ideal.

It helps to be specific. For example, one husband fantasized having more independence by taking more time to work on his hobby, building a telescope. The couple considered *how often* he wanted to work on the hobby, *how long* each hobby session should be and *where* the work was to take place. After answering these specific questions, the couple agreed to allot the husband one hour three times per week in which he worked on his telescope in their garage. The couple then agreed to try out the new arrangement.

Don't Pull "Triggers"

Conflict usually doesn't come out of the blue. Generally, there are recognizable "triggers" that set it off. One way to prevent arguments and disagreements is to learn to recognize the triggers and divert possible arguments into more positive directions.

Triggers are individually meaningful—a certain look that shows the partner that you don't care or are bored, a particular whine of voice, a glare, a sudden withdrawal from the conversation, constant complaining or even discussion of a particular topic.

Early in our first year of marriage, Kirby and I discovered that we could not talk rationally about labor unions. That topic became a red flag for both of us, so we have never discussed labor unions since (though after twenty-plus years of marriage we probably could handle the strain now).

When we recognize a trigger for conflict, we should unashamedly avoid it. It is no disgrace to avoid almost certain conflict. It isn't necessary to stand boldly and spit in the eye of the tiger to demonstrate courage. To stay healthy, we avoid excess cholesterol, fatty foods, harsh sunshine and a sedentary lifestyle. To avoid injury, we avoid riding bikes down the center stripe of a two-lane street, tugging on Batman's cape and insulting Hulk Hogan.

If conflict is a temptation, flee from the temptation. Jesus admonished us to avoid temptation. "If your right eye causes you to sin, tear it out. . . . And if your right hand causes you to sin, cut it off" (Mt 5:29-30). That is, if you sin by touching, don't touch; if you sin by looking, don't look. Avoiding temptation is one way we resist the devil, who will then flee from us (Jas 4:7). Avoidance is often the "way out" of temptation that the Lord provides (1 Cor 10:13).

Besides avoiding trigger situations, use the triggers to remind yourself to be more loving. Plan ahead how you can deal with the triggers. Then let them be reminders to put your plan into action.

Three Methods

Couples successfully resolve conflict in many ways, but some ways are more likely than others to bring long-lasting solutions.

Similarly, some conflict-management styles are usually not helpful. When a spouse habitually *avoids* conflict or *gives in,* he or she is not likely to remain happy.

A *compromise* strategy, continually bargaining tit for tat, will keep the couple happy longer, but will not satisfy indefinitely. A compromise is like a tied football game. If the San Francisco Forty-Niners are ahead by three points with fifteen seconds to play and the Chicago Bears kick a field goal, the Bears are happy with the tie, but the Niners are sad. The next week, if the Bears are tied in the final minutes by the Atlanta Falcons, the Bears may be disappointed. The following week, Denver ties the Bears. Week after week, the string continues. The Bears will soon be looking for a new coach.

Of course, marriage conflict isn't like professional football—at least for most couples. An attitude of *winning* each conflict may make the winner happy for a while, but the loser is tough to live with and may make the victory costly in other ways.

Thus, the most productive way to handle conflict is to use a win-win strategy. Numerous authors explain ways to resolve conflict productively. For example, Norm Wright suggests nine steps to successfully resolving conflict:

1. Recognize conflict issues.
2. Listen carefully to the other person.
3. Select the most appropriate time to discuss the conflict.
4. Communicate in such a way to make it easy for your partner to respond; for example,
   a. Speak for yourself, not for your spouse.
   b. Document your opinions with descriptive behavioral data.
   c. Describe your feelings.
   d. State your intentions.
5. Define the conflict issue or problem that requires a specific solution.
6. Identify your own contribution to the problem.
7. Identify alternatives.
8. Decide on a mutually acceptable solution.
9. Implement new behaviors.[7]

John Gottman and his colleagues propose another approach.[8] They suggest that the couple begin their attempt to resolve conflict by having a *gripe time.* Each partner states his or her complaint, and then they work together to turn the gripes into specific problems that are (at least in principle) solvable. Second, the spouses *set an agenda* for their discussion: they decide on the one or two most important things they will discuss. In the *problem-solving* stage, the couple changes the two specific gripes into specific positive suggestions.

Gottman and his coauthors and Wright give clear guidelines for carrying out their suggestions. However, sometimes the couple trying to implement the suggestions must feel like a cartoon I once saw. Two scientists stand in front of a blackboard with scientific scrawls trailing systematically from upper left to lower right. In the middle of the blackboard, interrupting the equations, is a dotted line connecting the top ten and bottom ten equations. Beside the dotted line are the words, "A miracle occurs here." One scientist points at the words and says, "I think you could be a little more explicit at that point."

Wright's step eight, "Decide on a mutually acceptable solution," and Gottman et al.'s problem-solving stage both smack of a miracle, even though they take pains to show how to arrive at a mutually acceptable solution or solve problems.

Roger Fisher and William Ury, in *Getting to Yes: Negotiating Agreement Without Giving In,* suggest a more specific way to achieve a win-win situation.[9] They advise spouses to avoid becoming locked into rigid statements of position, such as "Your mother cannot come to live with us" and "She can, too; it's as much my house as it is yours." Statements of position are usually mutually exclusive. Either one person will win, or both will need to compromise.

Fisher and Ury point out that partners in conflict are actually trying to protect their interests rather than achieve victory on a specific position. Thus, if each partner identifies the interests behind the positions, it might be possible to devise a solution that will meet both partners' interests. Both will win, neither will lose and neither will have to compromise.

For example, Samuel didn't want Teresa's mother to live with them. After reflection, he said that his interests were (1) concern that his and Teresa's intimacy would be strained by having to attend to Tanya's mother so much, (2) loss of space in their already too cramped house and (3) the threat that Teresa's mother would compete with Samuel for her affection. Teresa identified her main interests as (1) concern that her mother was getting old and had no one who could look after her in the city where she lived, (2) a belief that extended family ties are important and that closer ties with her mother could help Samuel and Teresa to feel even more connected to each other and (3) a need to feel that Samuel valued her opinions and wishes.

After listing their interests, they realized that both of them wanted to preserve their marriage and avoid threats to that relationship. They brainstormed to find ways to meet both sets of needs. One suggestion was to move Teresa's mother to a nearby nursing home. Another was to convert the small apartment behind their house into a room for Teresa's mother. A third was to look for another older adult nearby with whom Teresa's mother could share a house. All three solutions were acceptable to both Samuel and Teresa, so they suggested them to Teresa's mother.

Besides employing Fisher and Ury's method to resolve differences, the healthy couple can also heed the advice of Elizabeth Jones and Cynthia Gallois, who, in 1989, published an analysis of couples' problem-solving rules.[10] The rules were grouped by using a statistical technique that detected similarities. Rules in each grouping are listed on table 4.

Generally, the partners tried to be considerate and positive with each other while disagreeing. They considered honest but sensitive self-expression to be essential to negotiating a solution that was mutually satisfying. Finally, they employed rationality and specific problem solving rather than emotional outbursts and general accusations and complaints.

In summary, a healthy marriage will inevitably run into conflicts, but spouses usually can work out their disagreements. The many principles for negotiating agreement may be boiled down simply into easy-to-remember guidelines:

1. Remain positive and considerate.

2. Deal with specific complaints and solutions.

3. Go for a win-win solution by concentrating on meeting the interests behind the complaints.

Table 4. Rules for marital conflict (from Elizabeth Jones and Cynthia Gallois, 1989).

Consideration
- ☐ Don't belittle, humiliate, or use character-degrading words about the other person
- ☐ Don't dismiss the other person's issue as unimportant
- ☐ Acknowledge and try to understand the other person's point of view
- ☐ Don't talk down to the other person; talk to him or her as an adult
- ☐ Don't blame the other person unfairly, or make unfair accusations
- ☐ Don't push your own point of view as the only right one; consider the other person
- ☐ Don't be sarcastic or mimic the other person
- ☐ Try to understand the other person's faults, and don't be critical or judgmental
- ☐ Don't hurt the other person
- ☐ Don't make the other person feel guilty
- ☐ Listen to the other person
- ☐ Don't talk too much or dominate the conversation
- ☐ Don't interrupt

Rationality
- ☐ Don't get angry
- ☐ Don't raise your voice
- ☐ Don't be aggressive or lose your temper
- ☐ Try and keep calm, and don't get upset
- ☐ Don't argue
- ☐ Don't bring up issues that tend to lead to arguments

Self-Expression
- ☐ Keep to the point; don't get involved in other issues
- ☐ Get to the point quickly
- ☐ Be honest and say what's on your mind
- ☐ Be specific; don't generalize
- ☐ Clarify the problem
- ☐ Express your feelings about the topic
- ☐ Explain and justify events rather than deny their occurrence
- ☐ Be consistent
- ☐ Explain reasons for your point of view
- ☐ Don't exaggerate
- ☐ Think before you act, and don't make rash judgments

Conflict Resolution
- ☐ Explore alternatives
- ☐ Make joint decisions
- ☐ Explain reasons for your point of view
- ☐ Explain your feelings about the topic
- ☐ Be prepared to compromise
- ☐ Be able to say you're sorry
- ☐ Resolve the problem so that both people are happy with the outcome
- ☐ Explain and justify events rather than deny their occurrence

Positivity
- ☐ Try and relieve the tension in arguments (make appropriate jokes, laugh together)
- ☐ Use receptive body language (for example, open body position)
- ☐ Look at each other
- ☐ Be supportive and give the other praise where due
- ☐ Don't hurt the other person

Be Patient

When a highly conflicted marriage needs healing, problems loom like mountains that must be moved. If the mountain is to be moved successfully, faith is required.

The task seems insurmountable. The tools seem as ineffective as teaspoons. God seems so far removed that it feels hopeless to call on him.

Yet call on him we must. Jesus is the peacemaker. The first and most important step in healing is prayer, and healing will continue only with persistent prayer.

We need a vision of the landscape without the mountain. What would the marriage be like if conflict were healthy rather than destructive and unhealthy?

Recall that in marriages plagued by serious conflict, each spouse attributes the difficulty to the partner's recalcitrant personality. To change the marriage, the partners must ask themselves, How would I know if my spouse changed? Would I require perfection of him or her?

How would he or she behave? For how long? How many failures could I tolerate before I concluded that my partner's personality had not changed? These specific questions must be answered honestly if conflict resolution strategies are to change.

I have a plaque in my office. It says, "Life: By the mile it's a trial. By the inch it's a cinch." Forming new conflict-management strategies requires moving patiently, inch by inch, toward your goal.

Summary
Spouses must deal with their differences. If conflict persists and worsens over time, however, you and your partner are probably in a power struggle—disagreeing over who can say what the rules will be. To extricate yourselves from the power struggle, you must seek the grace to love and sacrifice for each other. To give this attitude a chance to grow,

☐ avoid conflict when possible,

☐ respect and value each other during necessary conflicts,

☐ be less concerned with complaining about your spouse's behavior than about increasing your own demonstrations of love,

☐ spend less time defining the problem than searching for a solution that will meet both partners' interests, and

☐ be patient with yourself and especially with your spouse.

In conflict, as with closeness and general communication, cultivate a positive vision and be eager to forgive each other when you fail to live up to the ideal.

10

Assigning and Accepting Responsibility

"**D**addy, why is Mommy crying?"

"She's feeling sad."

"But why is she feeling sad?"

"Things haven't been going very well for her lately, dear."

"Why?"

Putting down the dish towel, Conrad gave seven-year-old Lynne his undivided attention. "People haven't liked some of the things your mommy has done, and they've told her so."

Lynne placed a saucer in the dishwasher. "Why didn't they like what Mommy did?"

"Because they had other ideas about what should be done with some money that the school had." Conrad was always amazed at how frustrated he became when Lynne was in one of her inquisitive moods.

"Why'd they have different ideas?"

Conrad stifled the urge to become impatient. "Some people just look at life differently."

"Why?"

Arrggh, he thought. Suddenly, Conrad was overcome with a brilliant inspiration. "Because God made 'em different." *So there,* he thought.
"Why?"

Sometimes children are relentless in their questioning. But the fact is, we never get over that natural inquisitiveness. We want to know why this child was born into our family, or whether that illness was in God's will, or why we have marital tensions. Like Lynne, we are rarely satisfied with the answers.

In knowledge, there is some sense of control—even when control is objectively not present in a situation. Perry London once described a study by Ellen Langer of Yale University.[1] College students were invited to play the card game "War" against one of two opponents. One opponent was "The Snook," a man whose behavior suggested that he was too incompetent even to talk. His clothes were buttoned incorrectly, ketchup stains decorated his lapels and his suit was perma-wrinkled. The other opponent was "The Dapper," faintly reminiscent of "Bond, James Bond." The Dapper had a pencil-thin mustache, manicured nails and a three-piece suit. No doubt he spoke with a clipped British accent.

Objectively, "War" is a fifty-fifty win-loss game, strictly a matter of chance. Each opponent turns a card face up, and the highest card wins. If the two players happen to turn over cards of equal value, they each deal two more cards face down, and the third card face up. Whoever has the highest third card wins all the cards in play.

The students knew they were playing a game of pure chance, yet when asked to bet "play money" on the outcome, those who played against The Snook bet more money than those who opposed The Dapper. The knowledge of the opponent's physical appearance made the students *feel* as if they had more control.

Generally, knowledge works to our benefit. It helps us predict, control and understand futures that may determine our behavior. Information helps us perform better.

As Langer's Dapper and Snook study shows, though, sometimes our mind betrays us by providing an illusion of control rather than a true perception of control. We can deceive ourselves.

The Blessing and Curse of Causes

Humans constantly strive to determine the cause of events. If we think we know the cause, we feel more in control. In our efforts to predict events, however, we often attribute causality when none in fact exists. This is easiest to see in superstitious behavior. Much to his wife's discomfort, the baseball player on a hitting streak may not change his "lucky socks" for weeks. That's superstitious behavior.

We often attribute causality when it exists only occasionally. For instance, a child might find that asking Dad for special privileges is likely to be more successful than asking Mom. The child soon asks Dad every time he is available, even though Dad grants the special privileges only occasionally.

Life is an interminable effort to make predictions, so we describe our experience in terms of rules. It would seem that our best strategy would be to make the *most accurate* rules possible. But this turns out not to be the case. The world we live in is incredibly complex—too complex to allow us to make completely accurate rules. We therefore settle for general rules, which are inaccurate sometimes but accurate most of the time. Once we make a "rule," though, we *want* to believe our rule. Our minds perceive the evidence selectively, so that our general rule seems to be supported. It takes a lot to change our "rules," because we pay attention to supporting evidence but ignore, explain away or deny contradictory evidence.

Explanations of marital events are of several types: expectations, descriptions and attributions.

Our *expectations* create self-fulfilling prophecies. If we expect a child to misbehave, the child will usually accommodate our expectations. If we expect the child to behave, the child usually will. If we expect a spouse to complain continually, that will usually be the case. If we expect the spouse to be our devoted helper, that also will usually be true.

One may *describe* one's spouse to oneself (and sometimes to others) using positive trait labels such as *friendly, competent, happy, sweet, reliable, trustworthy, sexy, intelligent* and *fun to be with.* Or one may apply negative labels to the spouse: *critical, incompetent, sad, bitchy, unreliable, a snake, frigid, stupid* or *boring.* Inevitably, one comes to believe that the labels are accurate. Though in fact they are accurate at best only part of the time, gradually the spouse will likely begin to live up (or down) to one's expectations.

If you treat your mate as unreliable, you will, by your own behavior, push your mate in that direction.

If you view your marriage as largely positive, you are blessed. It will probably grow to be more positive over time. But if you view your marriage as negative, it will likely grow more negative unless you work hard to change it.

☐ Assess the way you describe your marriage. List the adjectives you would use to describe it.

☐ Assess your spouse. How would you describe him or her to someone else?

☐ Does that description change in the privacy of your own mind? If so, how?

Expectations and descriptions of one's marriage and one's spouse are only two kinds of causes of marital events. *Causal attributions* are explanations about why certain events happen.

☐ Assess the causal attributions in various aspects of your relationship.

☐ Is your spouse usually forgiving of you when you do something that hurts him or her? Why do you think he or she behaves this way?

☐ Is your spouse usually intimate with you? Why or why not?

☐ When your spouse needs more distance than you would like, what does your spouse do or say? Why?

☐ How well does your spouse communicate with you? When communication fails, why does it break down?

☐ Are you generally able to resolve conflicts with your spouse? When you cannot come to a friendly agreement on an issue and your spouse seems unwilling to bend, why do you think he or she is that way?

☐ Is your spouse likely to blame you for things that go wrong in your marriage, or is your spouse more likely to blame himself or herself? Or neither? Why do you think your spouse is this way?

☐ How committed is your spouse to making your relationship better? Almost everyone goes through ups and downs in commitment. When your spouse seems less committed to the relationship than at other times, why do you think this happens?

How you answered the "why" questions may reveal some things about your relationship. In general, happily married couples actually attribute the cause of their problems differently from unhappily married couples.

A partner in a distressed marriage tends to expect that the spouse's *positive* behavior is due to external, temporary and specific causes. For example, when Tim and Annette were arguing constantly, Annette went to counseling with her pastor one morning and felt she had a breakthrough. That afternoon, she made Tim a special meal and went out of her way to be nice to him. Tim thought, *She's just trying to get something. She probably feels guilty and this niceness won't last. It's just because we had the argument this morning.* His attributions led to accusations and another vicious argument, despite Annette's resolve to be different.

When distressed couples experience *negative* events, they usually explain the causes as global (rather than specific), due to the partner (rather than the self), due to the partner's (enduring) negative intent, and likely to persist or repeat.[2] When Tim forgot to pick up their nine-year-old from soccer practice, so that Annette had to drive across town through rush-hour traffic, she thought, *This is all his fault. I'll bet he did this on purpose. Forgot, huh? He's just irresponsible. He's done this a thousand times before, and he'll probably do it another thousand times.*

Happy couples tend to view *positive* events as due to global causes, stable, praiseworthy and intentional. *Negative* events are viewed as specific, unstable and unintentional.

☐ Evaluate the attributions of causality you wrote down previously. In each case, was the attribution specific or global? Stable or temporary? Worthy of praise or blame? Intentional or unintentional?

How you and your spouse handle expectations, descriptions and causal attributions is important to other areas of your marriage. Return to figure 2 (in chapter five) and use the Marriage Thermometer to rate how you consider cause and responsibility in your marriage.

Thinking About Causes

Look at the picture of the old woman in figure 4. Can you see a wart on her nose?

Perhaps you've seen the drawing before. Originally published in the 1930s in a humor magazine, it appears in most textbooks in introductory psychology. If you are familiar with the picture, you know that it contains pictures of both an old woman and a young one.

Look again. Can you see both? Studies have shown that people who

Figure 4.

are told to look for an old woman will usually see her before they see the young woman. We usually see what we look for.

Now that you know a young woman and an old woman are contained within the single drawing, try an experiment. Look at the picture for about a minute and think about your experience.

Could you see both an old and a young woman at precisely the same time, or did your mind flip-flop from one to the other? When you began the experiment, even though you knew both pictures were contained in the drawing, did you have more difficulty seeing one picture than the other? As you continued to examine the picture, did it become easier to perceive one, then the other, or did you continue to see one picture more easily than you did the other?

To help you derive lessons that can make your marriage better, I want to take you on a brief excursion into experimental psychology. In particular, we will examine how perception and memory operate.

Perception

All marriages contain two pictures. The positive picture contains the reasons you married your spouse, the things he or she does that are interesting, the benefits of marriage, the comfort of getting to know another person intimately. The negative picture contains the aggravations, your spouse's bad habits, the memories of the poor interactions you've had, the tensions and costs of the relationship.

As in your experience with the old woman-young woman, if you are like most people (1) you can perceive only one picture at a time, (2) you have more trouble seeing one picture than seeing the other, at least at first, and (3) as you practice, you can more easily flip-flop from one picture to see the other.

When you first marry, you make a commitment to your spouse. Your mind wants consistency. The import of your commitment overshadows other perceptions, blotting out the negative picture of the spouse. It is as if the mind had a spotlight with which it illuminates certain actors while leaving others in the shadows.

As your marriage continues, you accumulate experiences. New memories are formed, and the spotlight shifts, illuminating new actors. Are the new actors the Laurence Oliviers, the Dustin Hoffmans, the Meryl Streeps, or are they villains and hacks, memorable because of their incompetence?

Memory

When the spotlight shifts, though, not only are new actors highlighted, but old actors are relegated to the shadows and the wings. It isn't just that you forget, that you do not play the old videotapes. The mind's drive for consistency is extremely powerful. The mind actually remakes the videotape so that you "remember" a memory that in fact never happened. You truly see old experiences in a new light.

It's a remarkable fact. We never remember past experiences accurately. Rather, we re-create new memories.[3]

Most people use something like a videotape analogy to think of memory. They reason that when an event happens, the mind videotapes it and records the sights, sounds and smells. When the event ends, the videotape is filed in the giant library called the brain. To remember an event, we dispatch our attention to search for the proper videotape. Sometimes the videotape is poorly labeled and is not easily retrievable. Perhaps it is so poorly labeled that it is totally lost to memory, or perhaps it is recovered only years later, when we stumble across the videotape in another context. This analogy, though, is inaccurate in important ways.

In my introductory psychology classes, I conduct a memory exercise based on a classic study by W. F. Brewer. I read twelve sentences, instructing the students to recall the sentences *word for word*. The sentences may include the following:

The graduate assistant was dumb.

The absent-minded professor lost his keys.

The student's parents sent bail money to him.

The python caught the mouse but did not eat it.

The bullet struck the bull's-eye.

The taxi driver did not like people from other countries.

After reading all the sentences, I place sentence stems on the overhead projector to prompt my students. Without looking back, try now to complete the sentences *exactly* as they were stated on the previous page.

The graduate assistant _____ .
The absent-minded professor _____ .
The student's parents _____ .
The python _____ .
The bullet _____ .
The taxi driver _____ .

Now check your memory against the *exact* wording. The mistakes that are made are more instructive than are correct answers. For example, according to some students, the poor professor who lost his car keys actually had a variety of difficulties. "The absent-minded professor forgot his car keys." "The absent-minded professor left his car keys in his car." "The absent-minded professor didn't have his car keys." "The absent-minded professor misplaced his car keys." Some even realized that the professor didn't really lose his *car* keys at all; he lost his *keys*. (The word *car* was not in the original sentence.)

The students' mistakes, and possibly yours, reveal that long-term memory (memory over a minute or longer) is actually *reconstructive*. We remember the gist of the event and then make up the specifics to be consistent with the important kernel of memory. Our experience of memory, though, is that we are actually remembering *exactly* what took place.

A little reflection will confirm this reconstructive understanding of memory. If every event we ever experienced were recorded in minute detail in our minds, the connections available to store the memory would be exhausted in a couple of years. Our brain is an amazing creation of God, but its capacity is still limited.

Consider a woman recently widowed. As she remembers her marriage, her memory is probably highly influenced by the trauma of her husband's death. That death wrested something precious away from her. Her mind wants consistency, so her memories are elaborated consistently with the events that are most powerfully on her mind—those surrounding the death. As a result, a widow has a tendency to idealize the memories of her marriage. She honestly recalls primarily the good times, though if she concentrates on it, she can recall some of the less pleasant times.

Now consider the recent divorcee. As she remembers her marriage, her memory is also likely to be influenced by the recent trauma, the divorce. The divorce is painful instructor to her mind in elaborating on the memories of her marriage that are consistent with the separation. She will probably recall more of the negative interactions with her ex-spouse than the positive—though, if she concentrates on it, she can recall some of the pleasant times too.

The implication is that the general emotional tone of any marriage actually shapes our memory of the marriage. For the happily married spouse, it isn't just a matter of consciously overlooking bad experiences. Memories are actually different from what they would have been in a negatively toned marriage. If negative events pile up and conflicts become intense, the spouse will automatically reconstruct the past to be consistent with those recent events.

Principles for Change

Based on our knowledge of memory, here are some suggestions for improving your marriage. First, events and *actions* powerfully shape memories. Our memory of our behavior is usually better than our memory of our thoughts. Thus, to improve your marriage, *behave* as positively as possible as often as possible. You will simultaneously show yourself and your spouse that you love him or her, and you will implant that knowledge in your memories.

Second, the context within which you think about memories shapes the memories. If you examine your past while you are in a negative frame of mind, then the next time you recall that memory, it will actually be more negative than it was previously. Thus, to improve your marriage, look at the positive, try to think of negative behavior in as positive a light as possible, and avoid reviewing your marriage while in an

146 ———————————————————————————— *Hope for Troubled Marriages*

overall negative frame of mind.

Third, we can direct and discipline our minds. A satisfying marriage is enhanced when spouses actively try to keep their attributions positive. Focus on your goals. Set your sights on improving your marriage.

Fourth, focus on your own responsibilities rather than those of your spouse. Confess your part in hurtful relationships, and avoid blaming your spouse.

Fifth, focus on the close times rather than the times of distance and separateness. Recall the warmth of togetherness, the security of emotional support. Don't dwell on any times of cold estrangement if you can avoid it.

Sixth, focus on the good communication rather than the bad. Think of the times you've "clicked," and strive to duplicate those.

Seventh, when conflict over differences arises, focus on problem solving rather than naming and blaming. Don't merely use the differences to confirm a negative perception of the marriage's direction. Rather, use differences as a stimulus to grow together in a new direction.

Eighth, place credit for your thriving relationship where it belongs: the sustaining hand of God and your efforts to bring about the vision of marriage he gave you.

Preventing Additional Problems

Preventing marital problems from becoming larger requires eliminating harmful attributions of cause and replacing them with conscious consideration.

Attribution therapy helps people change their understanding of what is causing their behavior. We might naively think that this could be accomplished simply by telling a person to think differently, but we'd be wrong. Telling people to think differently rarely changes the way they think about their marriage.

Marla blamed her spouse for all their communication problems. When the counselor asked Marla whether she had any responsibility for their problems, she said, "Of course I'm partly responsible."

"Which part is your responsibility?" asked the counselor.

"I—uh—ah—well, at least half," she said.

Marla endorses the concept that most marital problems are not one-sided, but she believes it only in the abstract. And she doesn't live her life in the abstract. She lives it in moment-by-moment actions. In her daily living she believes, and acts as though she believes, that all the couple's problems are James's fault.

A naive counselor can never change the beliefs that are actually guiding Marla's life by telling her, "Marital problems are half your responsibility." Before she will change her beliefs, Marla must somehow be *shown* how she is helping create problems.

Counseling techniques are generally designed to help people see specifically how they are contributing to marital tensions and to motivate them to change those ways. It is difficult for you, while reading a book, to see how you might need to change, because your mind is already aimed in a particular direction. I can't just *tell* you, like the naive counselor, that you should consider different causes for any problems you might have. Perhaps I could convince you in the abstract that you could view your marriage differently than you now do, but unless your changed beliefs touch the specific daily decisions of your life, changing your beliefs in the abstract will do little good.

Let me suggest some self-discovery exercises that may help you understand your marriage in new ways.

1. Question yourself. Whenever you feel the painful sting of hurtful words, ask yourself, *Am I sure he (or she) meant to hurt me? Could there be other reasons that he (or she) wasn't sensitive to me? Maybe I'd better ask.*

2. Observe data you've been missing. Look for signs of tenderness you may usually ignore.

A husband and wife were discussing their troubled marriage. The husband described his loss of feeling for his wife. Then the wife began to relate a series of times when she had felt particularly hurt by her husband's neglect. As she became more emotionally wrapped up in her narrative, the husband reached his foot over and began, apparently absent-mindedly, to stroke her leg with his foot.

The alert counselor stopped their discussion and pointed out his behavior. "You say you feel nothing for your wife, but when she became distressed just now, you instinctively reached out to comfort her." Neither the husband nor the wife had paid attention to his gesture, yet this provided strong evidence to both that there was still contact between them.

Wrapped up in their own world, telling their story so long that they had begun to believe it, the partners had ignored important data. That simple incident helped the couple rediscover their connection with each other.

3. Look for the flip side of painful emotions. Our emotions are complex and often confusing. We try to make them comprehensible by labeling them with words. In labeling, we oversimplify.

Usually, anger and hurt are woven intricately together like a close plaid. When I see partners who are expressing lots of anger toward each other, I immediately look for the hurt underneath. Thus, when you see your spouse expressing anger, ask yourself, *How have I hurt her (or him)?* Instead of attributing the angry behavior to a desire to destroy you, think of it as a self-protective response to hurt. You might be able to ease the anger and the pain by looking for the flip side.

This also holds true for expressions of distress. When a spouse expresses hurt and distress, I usually want to know if he or she is also angry. Anger usually comes when a need, want or goal is blocked. As spouse, I should help my partner try to meet his or her needs, wants and goals. Letting distress lead me to ask about my spouse's needs helps tell me what I might do to relieve the distress.

4. Meditate on Ephesians 5:21—6:9. Read this passage, trying to put aside whatever you might have been taught about being the head of the house, being submissive or being within God's plan for the family. Consider this as possibly the main point of the passage: In whatever role you find yourself—husband or wife, parent or child, master or slave—your task as a Christian is to lay down your life for the other person. If we can have that attitude, the mind of Christ elaborated in Philippians 2:5-8, then we will usually be able to get past blaming.

In addition, when you read this passage, ask yourself what Paul's emphasis was. Was it the *rights* of headship, or was it the *responsibilities* of headship?

5. *Create an attitude of acceptance.* Larry Crabb suggests that three elements are needed to create an attitude of acceptance. Spouses must minister to each other's needs. They must acknowledge their own feelings, though they may not always act on the feelings. Finally, they should forgive each other's debts. With this attitude of loving our spouse despite his or her imperfections and failings, we practice true Christianity. We love others because God first loved us, giving his Son for us while we were yet sinners.

Solving Serious Problems

Minimizing negative attributions in a troubled marriage requires a willingness to suspend negative judgments, continued demonstrations of love and faithfulness, a determined effort to see the positive, and a healing of memories.

Partners in a troubled marriage tend to make stable negative evaluations of the marriage. Further, whenever the partner does something positive, the spouse explains it away, and whenever the spouse does something negative, the partner says, "I knew it." If the marriage is to be healed, the spouses must bury the hatchet. They must meet each other's successes with acceptance, and failures must be met with forgiveness, or at least with a wait-and-see attitude.

It isn't easy to break habitual thought patterns, but it can be done if spouses are determined. The negative thoughts of a troubled marriage are self-fulfilling prophecies. They bring about the very thing that they expect.

When we watch a movie like *Star Wars* or read a novel like C. S. Lewis's *Perelandra,* we willingly suspend our disbelief and become involved in the story. If we keep the critical part of our mind operating, we won't enjoy the movie or novel. But if we enter the framework of the story, we allow ourselves to derive pleasure and perhaps even enrichment from the experience. Even though we suspend our disbelief, we don't criticize ourselves for being taken in, duped or deceived by the author. We don't worry that somehow we will become unable to disengage ourselves from the experience.

Similarly, to change the way you view your troubled marriage, you must enter a more positive frame of reference. You must suspend any belief that the spouse isn't trying to work on the marriage or that improving the marriage is hopeless. Blame must be put aside. Give your spouse credit for his or her efforts, and suspend your speculations about his or her motivations. Let the actions speak, rather than your perception of your spouse's motivation.

Dealing with blame is a crucial aspect of improving marriage. The problem is especially difficult if one spouse appears to be the culprit. Perhaps one spouse has had an affair, beats the children, drinks incessantly or appears not to care about the relationship. When the spouse is flagrantly sinning, it is particularly hard to set blame aside.

When family members and friends hear of your marital troubles or sense that you are under stress, they may call to offer support. It is natural for you to describe some of your difficulties to them. Yet regardless of how objective you may try to be in describing the troubles, you still see things from your point of view, so your description of the troubles will be slanted. Because your friend is talking to you and is sympathetic to you, he or she will guide conversation in ways that support your point of view, too.

When family members and friends become involved in marital difficulties—even if the involvement is as simple as providing emotional support, which may be helpful—it becomes more likely that the couple will divorce.

My advice is to avoid discussing your marital problems with friends and relatives when that discussion involves complaining and recounting your spouse's wrongs. You'll be most tempted to discuss marriage problems with friends when you are hurt or angry. Remember, anger usually lurks beneath the hurt, and anger will persuade you to justify presenting your side of the troubles. You may tell yourself that you need wise counsel from a friend when what you really want is for your friend to proclaim you a righteous victim of your horrid spouse.

Consider carefully before you seek a friend's counsel. Seek counsel, as much as possible, when you are not feeling hurt or angry. Steer clear of describing the details of your interactions with your spouse. Seek prayer from your friend, knowing that he or she does not really need knowledge of the details to pray effectively. Jesus knows what happened.

On the other hand, friends can play an important role in helping heal your marriage if they (and you) steer clear of gossip. They can listen to you and validate you as a valuable person, help meet intimacy needs while tensions exist with your spouse, hear your confessions, help you understand things from a different perspective, pray for and with you, offer valuable emotional support, help you make decisions, help you think of productive actions, hold you accountable for carrying out positive plans and talk with you about your successes and failures.

Criticizing your spouse to others is only one danger to avoid. Don't criticize your spouse to yourself either. Larry Christenson suggests that whenever you find yourself criticizing your spouse, you should become "empathetically repentant"—that is, begin to examine your own life for the flaw you are finding in the other.[4] "She's selfish. She only wants her own way," the husband might say. But it should take little prayerful reflection for him to find ample evidence of the same motivations in his own life. His own sincere repentance should leave him little time or motivation to criticize his wife.

Sometimes, couples will deal with their troubles successfully, yet they cannot seem to forget the past. It always lurks like a specter on the edge of consciousness. Perhaps a public ceremony would help them leave the past behind. Many couples go through a second wedding ceremony to mark important changes. Some marriage enrichment programs, like Marriage Encounter, close their weekend marathons with a marriage ceremony.

Other ceremonies might also be meaningful. Some of my clients have written their complaints about their marriage as part of the initial assessment. After successfully completing marital therapy, they burned copies of their complaints as a symbolic gesture that the complaints were forever in their past and would not be brought up in the future.

Jay Haley, a noted family therapist from Washington, D.C., tells of a husband and wife who had both been involved in affairs. After successful marital therapy, they wanted some powerful ritual to signify a new start. Because of the particularly hurtful level of their former interactions, they opted for a rather drastic symbolic act. They both cut off their hair: the man shaved his head, and the woman cut her hair no longer than one inch all over her head. They entombed the hair scraps in a box and buried that "casket" in the desert as a symbol of the death of their old marital habits.[5]

Finally, the couple needs a healing of memories. A variety of psychologists and even ministers have suggested that Jesus is a healer of memories. They suggest that individuals imagine vivid fantasies in which Jesus is invited to heal the memory of the rift between spouses.

Concerned about the New Age mentality, some people are justifiably careful about imagery methods. Based on our discussion at the beginning of the present chapter about the nature of memory, we can see, though, that God has provided a natural way for memories to be reshaped. If we ask the Lord to heal our memories, he can and will do it. Memories are not like imperishable videotapes of experience. They are subject to re-creation with each recall. If we bring those memories under the blood of Jesus, they can be washed as white as snow.

Summary

It's natural to blame one's spouse for most marital difficulties. Partners' failures to forgive each other, experience closeness, communicate productively or resolve conflicts create a negative environment. And that environment makes it easier to expect more negative behavior, apply degrading trait-labels to the spouse, and blame the spouse for everything that goes wrong.

If this kind of negative environment has been established in your marriage, you can break out of it only with great effort. Strive to focus on the positive and examine your own responsibilities. Behave in ways your spouse will interpret as loving, even if you don't feel loving at the time. Pray that Jesus will heal your memories. Then your relationship can grow toward the ideal God wants for it.

11

Commitment

Hanged without ceremony on a foggy morning. Dietrich Bonhoeffer died alone on a prison gallows as a few men and a crowd of heavenly witnesses looked on. Malcolm Muggeridge, in *A Third Testament,* quoted a prison doctor who observed the event.

> I saw Pastor Bonhoeffer, before taking off his prison garb, kneeling on the floor praying fervently to his God. I was most deeply moved by the way this lovable man prayed, so devout and so certain that God heard his prayer. At the place of execution, he again said a short prayer and then climbed the steps to the gallows, brave and composed. His death ensued after a few seconds. In almost fifty years that I worked as a doctor, I have hardly ever seen a man die so entirely submissive to the will of God.[1]

Bonhoeffer's martyrdom could easily have been prevented. In 1933 he went to a parish in England, but with Hitler's influence rising in Germany, he decided that his Christian duty was back in his homeland. In 1939, Bonhoeffer visited the United States. He was pressured to remain in relative safety there, but he demurred, saying that he would have no right to participate in the reconstruction of Christian life in Germany after the war if he did not return to Germany and suffer with other faithful Christians there.

Finally, during his imprisonment, he could have escaped but refused because an escape might have endangered his brother and uncle, who were also prisoners. As Muggeridge aptly summarizes Bonhoeffer's life, "he was a man with a strong desire to escape, but who chose deliberately not to, in order to keep his freedom."

Bonhoeffer's commitment to his faith and his Christian duty as he saw it gave him a freedom that neither prison walls nor death could remove. We can be sure that the crowd of heavenly witnesses that observed Bonhoeffer's death applauded his commitment.

Assessing Your Marriage Commitment

Commitment may involve several parts. Commitment to the marriage has to do with the permanence of the marital union and the likelihood of divorce. But partners may also be committed to making the marriage work smoothly, improving the marriage and fulfilling individual responsibilities within the marriage.

☐ Assess your and your spouse's commitment in each of the above areas.

According to psychologist Caryl Rusbult, commitment may be described by an equation. I have renamed the terms, but the components of commitment are Rusbult's.

Commitment + Contentment = Compounding Investments − Competitors

Each component affects marital commitment.[2]

Contentment depends on confession, closeness, communication, managing conflict and considering one's responsibility—the components we have considered in chapters six through ten. Contentment is related to commitment but differs in important ways from it.

Commitment depends on the investments partners make in their marriage. It's like investing money: the more money that is invested, the more the returns are multiplied. Investments in marriage are time and effort. High commitment to improving the relationship will yield greater happiness. High commitment to fulfilling responsibilities to the spouse will yield more trust.

Our investments create a bank balance. When the investment balance is high and positive, withdrawals—such as disagreements, hurts and stresses—may be made without causing alarm and anxiety about the health or permanence of the relationship. When the investment balance is close to zero or negative, though, the health and stability of the relationship may be threatened even if a withdrawal is hinted, and especially if a withdrawal is made.

☐ How high is your investment balance in your marriage? Is your relationship so positive that an occasional negative interaction is not very damaging? Or is your balance close to zero?

Other investments besides time and effort contribute to a marriage's stability. Things held in common between spouses cement commitment. Children, home ownership, joint bank accounts, business partnership, shared leisure activities and mutual friends can all increase commitment to a marriage.

☐ List the things held in common between you and your spouse. How important are these mutual investments to you? To your spouse?

Commitment to marriage also depends on the alternatives to the marriage. We may simultaneously be committed to God, career, friends, our own pleasure, avoidance of pain, children and many other things. By prioritizing our commitments, we make difficult value decisions easier, but at times, prioritizing gives way to immediate demands.

For example, many Christians would prioritize commitments as God first, family second and career third. Yet when a major project is due at work, we may put aside usual family time to deal with job demands. We carefully try to balance our priorities over the long haul.

Sometimes, commitment to certain activities or people threaten commitment to a marriage. Affairs commonly break up marriages. Perhaps as common, though, are commitments to volunteer work (such as youth sports or PTA), working long hours or involvement in social or even church groups.

☐ Do you feel that you are too committed to some activities?

☐ Are those overcommitments creating tensions in your marriage?

☐ Are there activities in your spouse's life that you feel are too involving and are thus threatening your marriage relationship?

Competitors to the marriage relationship require time, effort and devotion. They can become a real problem. As a spouse expends energy on a competitor, both spouses begin to think differently about the competitor. The competitor is taken seriously as a challenger to the marriage commitment. As more attention is paid to the competitor, evidence is accumulated that the competitor indeed threatens the marriage. This cycle easily becomes a self-fulfilling prophecy if the partners do not make visible changes in their allocation of time.

☐ Do you consider any competitor to your marriage as a serious threat to your commitment, or your spouse's commitment?

☐ Are any activities so involving that they threaten your having time or energy to improve the relationship?

☐ Do any activities threaten your ability to carry out your marital duties?

Like each of the other aspects of marriage—confession and forgiveness, closeness, communication, conflict resolution and causal attributions—commitment is not isolated from the whole; it permeates each area. Each married couple must commit himself or herself to forgive, to strive to become closer, to communicate appropriately, to resolve conflicts, to accept responsibility where it is due and to exhibit commitment externally and internally. Commitment is the skin that holds the parts of the marriage together, so its condition and care are vitally important.

You have now considered the role of commitment in your relationship. Go back to figure 2 and use the Marriage Thermometer to rate the strength of commitment in your marriage.

The Changing Face of Commitment

As we approach the twenty-first century, many have lost the sense of commitment embodied in the marriage vows: "I take this person to be my lawfully wedded [spouse], to have and to hold, from this day forward, for richer and for poorer, in sickness and in health, until death do us part."

Commitment has come to mean a temporary trial. Recently I heard a person talking about her marriage commitment. She said, "I was committed to him as a faithful spouse, but, well, it just didn't work out so we got a divorce. Now, I'm in another committed relationship, and we'll probably get married in a couple of years if our love lasts."

How far this is from the biblical concept of everlasting covenant! The committed couple can bolster their commitment to each other by studying the concept of covenant and integrating that understanding with their marriage. The vision of marriage directs the spouses' steps. Commitment is a bond that is forged in the privacy of the mind and tested publicly in the furnace of daily living.

Fairness, Rewards and Costs

Ideally, marital commitment is based on the marriage covenant. But today many people no longer understand the concept of covenant. For them, commitment depends on judgments made by spouses.

One theory suggests that commitment depends on each spouse's evaluation of whether the marriage is fair.[4] Supposedly, each person constantly asks whether the expected balance of rewards and costs matches the actual perceived balance. Further, partners compare their balance of rewards and costs to the balance of rewards and costs that their spouse is obtaining.

Such an understanding of commitment based on fairness explains a puzzling finding. How can a person remain committed to a marriage that is not very rewarding? Perhaps, although the marriage is not rewarding, it demands little of the spouse. Net rewards would still outweigh net costs. Further, if little is expected from the marriage, then the meager satisfaction wouldn't be disappointing. Finally, resentment wouldn't build if the partner wasn't getting much from the marriage either. Undoubtedly, some people maintain their marital commitment because of fairness considerations.

Another theory, though, holds that people remain committed only to relationships that are more rewarding than costly, regardless of how fair the relationship is perceived to be.[5] Undoubtedly, some people maintain their commitment due solely to considerations of reward.

These theories suggest that a couple could improve their commitment by (1) increasing the rewards of marriage, (2) decreasing the costs of marriage, (3) decreasing their expectations of the benefits of marriage and (4) keeping an equitable balance between spouses. Such theories presuppose that people are fundamentally utilitarian, evaluating their marital commitment only in light of their own needs. Such thinking is antithetical to the Christian worldview, which elevates self-sacrifice over individualism and places the good of others over the good of self. Nonetheless, even Christian partners need to establish a mutually rewarding relationship—not as the sole foundation of commitment but as one essential component of marital contentment.

Rusbult's Investment Theory

Remember Rusbult's equation: commitment is composed of marital contentment plus compounding investments minus competing alternatives. Thus, when partners are unhappy, their commitment is necessarily decreased, though (let's hope) not shattered. Commitment can grow as contentment is increased, investments are compounded and competing alternatives to marriage are decreased.

Growth may be promoted, then, by building more investments in the marriage. One important investment is children. Even though children have been shown to decrease *marital* satisfaction, they usually increase *family* satisfaction.[6] They certainly form a bond between the parents who share care and concern for the children and their development.

Other important investments are shared possessions, including bank accounts, pets, property, baths, beds, household responsibilities and space within the house.

Couples also share an identity as a couple, which is an investment in their marriage. Mutual friends interact with the partners as a couple. The couple is invited out together, referred to as husband and wife and generally treated as inseparable.

Couples may also invest their time and energy together. Some couples enjoy working together to decorate or remodel their house. Others like to share leisure activities such as camping, backpacking, playing tennis, going to the lake or mountains or traveling. Each investment strengthens commitment. Spouses wanting to help their commitment grow can creatively share their lives together.

The final element of the formula for increasing commitment is to decrease alternatives to the marriage.

Gray and Holly had been married for twelve years. Throughout the marriage, the story had been the same. Gray was a workaholic. His workaholism had strained their marriage from the beginning, when he called his office twice during the first day of their honeymoon.

Despite the strain, Holly and Gray enjoyed each other and had largely a positive relationship, marred occasionally by the workaholism. Gray had been the youngest assistant executive vice president at his manufacturing firm, and he had strained hard for advancement. Holly had clung to his promise that advancement would ease the pressure, but a year before they came to counseling, he had received the promotion. The pressure had not eased; it had escalated.

Holly was thoroughly dissatisfied. Both she and Gray were Christians and were committed to their marriage, so they were motivated to find answers. Why was Gray so *driven* to achieve? Could he ever change? How could Holly accept Gray more?

What makes a person work so hard?[7] Many things. Like other difficulties, workaholism comes in a variety of types. Most workaholics are generally happy people who immensely enjoy their work. In fact, they almost live for work and treat outside activities as a distraction.

Some workaholics are insecure people who earn love and security by their production rather than through their relationships. If they succeed at work, life is wonderful. If not, life is horrible.

Other workaholics have poor self-esteem, which, like an unscratchable itch, cannot be touched by work or by relationships. These workaholics do not value themselves. Because they need mental consistency, they seek unconsciously to provoke rejection in others, which confirms their poor self-esteem. Workaholism is one way to provoke rejection in a spouse. For the workaholic with poor self-esteem, workaholism can drive coworkers, employees and employers to distraction and lead to the unconsciously desired failure at work, too.

Other workaholics have high energy levels. They wake early and seem to need less sleep than others. Instead of being psychologically depleted by stress, they seem to thrive on it— the more the better. Without stress, they become grouchy and sometimes physically ill. These workaholics have a high capacity to manage their lives well. They throw boundless energy into marital and family relationships, friendships and even volunteer organizations. Their workaholism is a style of life that usually benefits many people, though it may eventually wear out the workaholics themselves.

Regardless of the motivation, though, workaholics share several commonalities. They are usually intense, driven, competitive, energetic and goal-oriented. They tend to spend more time with work than with family, though they can put their workaholism to good use within the family too. They often bring the same intensity to family life as to work— driving, scheduling, controlling and goal-orienting their spouse and children. Thus, most workaholics usually require people to adjust to them more than they are able to adjust to others.

Helping Gray and Holly involved first assessing their particular situation. Gray seemed to be the type of workaholic who is insecure and earns love and approval through his work. With any workaholic, the first decision is usually whether living with the person is worth the price. Holly was committed to the marriage, so her decision in that regard was easy. For others, the decision is not so easy. The workaholic may, like an alcoholic or drug addict, be able to control his or her behavior, but it's likely that he or she will not change drastically. Rather, most of the change will usually be made by the spouse. Instead of clinging to unrealistic fantasies that she could reform Gray, Holly accepted that she would probably need to make most of the changes in the relationship.

Holly tried to assure Gray of her love frequently, to give him a sense of worth. She and Gray talked seriously about the problem, and she told him she needed more support from him. She asked him to state aloud his commitment to trying to meet her needs. In asking for an open commitment, Holly used Gray's need for consistency by helping him try to be consistent with his stated commitment to her. Gray was willing, especially as he began to see the marriage as an area in which he actually could achieve.

Holly, however, did not count on Gray's complete success. She also prepared herself for the testing that she anticipated. She knew that Gray would probably fail in his resolutions, especially when the pressure was greatest. So she planned to obtain support by establishing a confiding friendship in her women's Bible study.

Holly and Gray discussed ways to deal with Gray's relapses back into workaholism. His failures were treated more as a problem to solve than as a moral failure, which eased his guilt and contributed to positive relations and productive solutions.

Holly, too, made many changes. She tried to develop an interest in some of Gray's interests, such as management. She read books on business and time management—and learned some things that helped her manage her household better. She also streamlined her work around the house rather than continuing to expect Gray to pitch in and help more. Gray was eager to use some of the extra money he made to pay for a maid to help with the housework. Holly also began to find ways to be involved in Gray's work schedule. She went with him regularly on business trips, and they scheduled lunch together each Wednesday.

In one area, Holly was adamant. She insisted on three weeks of vacation each year. Further, Gray imposed his own limits on phone calls during vacation. He allowed himself three the first day, two the second, one the third and none after that.

For their marriage to get back on track, both Holly and Gray had to change. Holly was willing to make the most changes, as is usual with spouses of workaholics, but Gray, too, had to learn to be more flexible and to make sacrifices.

Dealing with Infidelity

How do you respond when your marriage is challenged by the betrayal of adultery?

Peggy and Steve got a divorce yesterday. Over two years, Steve had coasted into an affair with his coworker Melissa, and Peggy simply couldn't forgive him for that betrayal.

Steve described his initial "readiness for an affair." Although he had criticized others who had succumbed to sexual temptation, he later said, "I just felt unsettled in marriage. Even though I didn't mean to, I must have given off signals to every woman I met that I could be had."

Melissa was transferred into Steve's division from the St. Louis branch office. "It was excitement upon our first meeting. When I shook hands with her, I felt a thrill of sexual excitement. I began to have sexual fantasies about her. I was attracted to her physically because she was so many things that Peggy wasn't. Melissa was buxom, a little secretive, and always seemed like she enjoyed being a little 'bad.' Peggy was steady and dependable, but our sex life had never been that spectacular.

"At first, I joked around with Melissa, teasing and hinting about sexual things. Later, I started to arrange opportunities to meet with her alone for innocent reasons and enjoyed nonsexual touches."

Steve, thirty-nine, glanced over at the picture of the attractive thirty-year-old woman he had become infatuated with. Her smile was impish, and a mischievous glint graced her eye. "Then we began to stay late and work together. I had heard that Melissa led a wild nightlife, but that didn't seem to matter. If anything, it gave me a false sense of security. I thought I'd never really do anything wrong with a woman who seemed to be in the fast lane sexually.

"But it didn't turn out that way. We began to work late more often, and then afterward we would go out for something to eat. Lots of times I'd drive her home after we had eaten."

Steve sighed. His eyes seemed focused inward, and a gentle smile melded with the crinkles of worry lines as he recalled that time. "It was stressful for me. I knew that I was doing wrong, but I kept saying that nothing was happening except friendship. Peggy started to become jealous because I was spending so much time away from home, but I could look her in the eye and truthfully say that nothing was happening—nothing sexual, that is."

He sighed again and looked at the picture of his two sons. "Of course, that didn't last long. We started hugging, and soon it was kissing on the cheek when I took her home. Then one night, she gave me a real passionate kiss and invited me in. I just couldn't say no. I knew I should, and I knew she really didn't care about me. But I felt myself getting older, and I guess I needed some adventure.

"We made love that night, and she did things with me sexually that I had never even dreamed of. After that, I was just like her little puppy, following her for whenever she wanted to pat me on the head again.

"It couldn't last, of course. After about two months, she broke it off. If she hadn't, I guess I'd still be following her around.

"After the shock of the breakup, I could see how stupid I'd been. I'd done wrong and knew it. Finally, I went to Peggy and told her about the affair. I told her it was over. She was upset, but she said she forgave me. She lied.

"My life didn't seem worth living after that. I think she brought up the affair every day. She got angry and yelled at me about the affair in front of the kids. She told everyone we knew what a jerk I was. Then she got depressed, and every time she cried, it condemned me. After two years, I had been punished about as much as I could take. I gave her an ultimatum—that we go to counseling or I would leave. We went to counseling, but that didn't help. As far as she was concerned, the counselor was just another person to complain to weekly about my infidelity.

"Anyway, it was bad for us. Finally, *she* moved out. She said she couldn't stand to see my cheating face ever again. Now we're divorced."

Steve pulled his wallet from his back pocket and flipped it open to the pictures. He showed me Peggy's picture, holding the shoulders of their ten-year-old as she stood beside a younger Steve, who had his arm around their thirteen-year-old boy's shoulders. "I messed up. But I just wish she could have forgiven me. I still love her."

Adultery and Infidelity

Adultery is performing a sexual act outside of marriage. As such it usually damages or destroys a marriage, and it usually produces guilt in all people involved—the offending spouse, the injured spouse, the third member of the triangle, and even children and relatives. Usually, adultery produces jealousy in the injured party. Adultery is always sin.

Infidelity is broader than adultery. Infidelity is a breach of trust within the marriage. It might involve violation of any agreement, tacit or explicit, of the partners. The best way to determine whether an infidelity has occurred is to ask your spouse. An emotional response will tell you quickly whether an infidelity has occurred.[8]

One couple came to counseling because the wife had gone to lunch with a male coworker. Was the husband unreasonably jealous at this public act of friendship that obviously involved no sexual overtones? No. Husband and wife had always dealt honestly with each other and had agreed not to tempt themselves by having private liaisons with coworkers. The infidelity—the breach of trust—was the wife's failure to tell the husband of her wish to go to lunch and to discuss the request.

Types of Affairs

Psychotherapist Frank Pittman, who has had much experience in counseling couples whose marriages have been rocked by infidelity, identifies four types of affairs.[9] *Accidental infidelity* is an affair that results mostly from the offending spouse's tenuous commitment and values. He or she reacts to a tempting situation by giving in to the sexual pressures.

In the *romantic affair,* two people fall in love and close out external reality. The romantic affair usually happens at a crisis point in the life cycle. This kind of affair usually does not last long, but it is highly disruptive to a marriage.

Occasionally, an affair may be part of the *marriage arrangement.* Usually such affairs occur because the married couple cannot handle intimacy problems directly, so they limit intimacy by having external relationships. These affairs are most difficult on the "other woman" or "other man," who may remain in the relationship for years, hoping that some day the lover will divorce the spouse. In reality, however, there is little chance that the affair can ever become a legal marriage.

Continuous, compulsive, secret infidelity happens only in about one-fifth of all marriages. Usually, the offending partner is a man who fears female control and prevents it by conquering other women. This person is generally not good at marriage because it requires honesty, mutual respect and self-sacrifice.

Contrary to some other secular psychotherapists, Pittman concludes that "it would seem inappropriate to consider any of this 'normal.' "[10]

What Are Affairs Like?

Of course, affairs differ depending on the type. In general, though, Pittman paints a gloomy picture of affairs—contrary to popular news tabloids, novels and movies. "Most affairs seem to involve a little bad sex, and a lot of time on the telephone," he observes.[11] He describes the typical "other woman" and "other man" as no sexier than the spouse, and often similar in looks to him or her. Further, he suggests that the choice of a partner in adultery is usually more neurotic than the choice of a marital partner. Although affairs involve sex, most have more to do with friendship or with the offending partner's ego.

The flames of affairs are usually fanned by secrecy. The conspiracy produces an emotional bond, drawing the couple together. The couple have all the intimacy of a close relationship without any of the daily responsibilities. Thus, reconciliation in a marriage can rarely occur if an affair is ongoing. Usually, once an affair is revealed, it stops. When the affair continues after it has been revealed, the prognosis for the marriage is poor.

A marriage in which an affair occurs is not necessarily doomed to failure, yet the damage is severe. An affair strains a marriage in the same way that overuse and abuse strain a muscle. Microscopic muscle tears add to visible muscle damage. If the muscle is to heal, scar tissue will be formed. Inevitably, scar tissue makes the muscle weaker and more brittle than it was before the injury. Similarly, after an affair, the marriage is usually more weakly bonded and more brittle than it had been.

Healing for the Injured Partner

Having learned of an affair, the spouse is usually shocked, hurt and disoriented. This person usually feels guilty, thinking that he or she might have provoked the affair or could have done something to prevent it.

One of the first steps in healing is for the injured spouse to realize that he or she is not responsible for the affair. This is not to say that the spouse is guilt-free. There may be severe marital problems that are at least partly due to the spouse's behavior. Yet, regardless of those problems, the offending partner was never forced to deal with the problems by adultery. He or she is completely responsible for that choice.

Another step in healing is for the injured spouse to examine himself or herself for things that *are* his or her responsibility. Is there unforgiveness? It needs confession. Has he or she provoked the offending spouse to anger, denied him or her intimacy, fallen down in communication, engaged in constant conflict, blamed the spouse for all marital problems or been weak in his or her own commitment? The problems should be identified, repented of and confessed. Forgiveness should be sought and received.

The injured partner must decide whether he or she will remain committed to the marriage. Adultery is biblical grounds for divorce, though reconciliation is usually preferable.

If the marriage is to continue, the injured partner must struggle with trusting the spouse. Adultery and other infidelities are violations of trust, which is the fabric from which marriages are made. Rebuilding trust is a serious issue.

The injured partner usually must wrestle with jealousy over the affair. Pointless wondering whether the "other woman" or "other man" was sexier, more fun or a better lover will keep the injured spouse in turmoil and prevent the affair from being resolved and relegated to the past.

Finally, marital difficulties that preceded the affair must be resolved. In addition, the affair created additional difficulties, which also require resolution. Generally, it is difficult to resolve all these marital strains without some form of counseling. The affair is a public statement that the marriage is in trouble—if not before the affair, certainly after it. Those marital troubles must be attended to.

Healing for the Offender

The major problems for the unfaithful spouse are to accept responsibility for the affair, to forgive himself or herself and to rebuild trust.

When we have sinned, our strongest motivation is to justify ourselves. An unfaithful spouse may have excellent reasons that were used to justify entering an adulterous relationship—excellent reasons from his or her point of view. When the affair comes to light, he or she wants to maintain a sense of consistency. So blame and self-justification often abound.

If healing is to occur, the offending spouse must accept personal responsibility for his or her actions. Regardless of any provocation, adultery is only one of many ways that the provocation could have been handled. Provocations could have been handled by seeking counseling, by discussion, by angry conflict or by tearful recriminations. The choice made, however, was to have sex outside of the marriage covenant. The responsibility for that act is solely on the shoulders of the unfaithful partner, and it must be accepted.

Another step toward healing is that the unfaithful spouse forgive himself or herself. Pittman argues that more post-affair divorces are a result of the offender's not being able to handle the guilt of having betrayed the marriage than of the injured partner's being unable to forgive.[12] Thus, seeking and accepting forgiveness is essential to restoration of the marriage.

Finally, the one who has been unfaithful must patiently rebuild trust in the marriage. A serious violation of trust has occurred. Often, when the offender has confessed the affair and accepted forgiveness from the Lord and even from the spouse, he or she cannot understand why the injured spouse seems unwilling to resume the relationship. It's essential to realize that the violation of trust is one of the most damaging blows a relationship can receive, and the damage takes time to heal.

One danger is that the injured spouse will hold the affair over the unfaithful partner's head forever. That will prevent healing, just as continually placing pressure on a broken bone will prevent its healing. Rather, the injured spouse should decide on a time period during which the offender is "on trial." At the end of that period, the spouse should promise never again to mention the affair (unless, of course, the offender has another affair). Not talking about the affair will not completely heal the relationship, but it will allow the marriage to mend as well as it is able.

Even after the ravages of infidelity, marriages can and do heal.

Conclusion

At the beginning of chapter four, you wrote down a goal: "To make my marriage better than it is right now." If you have worked your way through the book to this point, you have taken a giant first step in bringing about that goal. You should congratulate yourself. As you use some of the suggestions here to increase your willingness to confess and forgive, to adjust closeness and distance, to communicate more productively, to solve problems without hurt, to avoid blame and to promote covenantal commitment, remember to congratulate yourself often on your effort.

All marriages have their ups and downs. Progress is never smooth. But if you continue to work at it, you can, with God's help, renew your love, value each other more and build a stronger, healthier marriage.

Epilogue
A Story of Two Trees

Two trees stood on a hill. One stood tall and straight. Its velvet leaves shimmered in the wind, revealing alternating soft and slick surfaces. Its trunk gleamed, and the birds nested within its full set of branches.

The second tree was shorter. Its branches and leaves were compact and sparse compared to those of the beautiful tree. Few birds nested among its leaves, but several bird families had made their homes in various holes in the trunk. The short tree's roots entwined themselves among the rocks and clawed at soil wherever it could be found.

"What's wrong with your trunk?" asked the beautiful tree.

"You mean this hollow section?" said the old tree. "This was from the fire of 1906. I went up in flames and thought I was a goner. Fortunately, the rains came and quenched the fire, leaving me at the edge of this meadow with a lovely view and many new friends like yourself."

"Thank you for the compliment," said the beautiful tree. "And why are you leaning to the side?"

"My lean allows me to see my roots more clearly," said the old tree. "It happened in 1936. A tornado came through here, ripping and tearing. I tell you, I was scared. All the beautiful young trees were tossed about and mangled. It was a tragic day. I almost met my Maker myself. If it hadn't been for that drought in 1925 that had made me extend my roots deep and wide, I'd have been killed for sure. It's kind of you to ask about me."

"I've always prided myself on my compassion," said the beautiful tree. "Excuse me, but I couldn't help but notice: you don't seem to spread much pollen around. You're not sick, are you? I'm not going to catch any disease from you, am I?"

The old tree laughed and shook its leaves hard. "No, I'm just getting old. I have been blessed with seeing many of my saplings raised. But sadly, many have also fallen. I've found that there are some things that I simply can't control in life. It has been difficult for me to adjust to. Thank you for being concerned about my health."

"It's nothing, really. Would you like for me to tell you about my history? It's fascinating."

"I would indeed," said the old tree and listened patiently for the next hour.

In the afternoon, a storm blew in from the west. The beautiful tree stood defiantly and righteously, awaiting its chance to pit its strength against the wind's. The old tree hunched its leaves together and thought of the painful events of the past and of the benevolence of its Maker.

When the wind swept through with terrible destructiveness, the beautiful tree was stripped of its velvet leaves, and its trunk cracked. "Why?" it asked the old tree.

"The Maker doesn't explain why," said the old tree. "The Maker just builds character."

Why does one marriage seem to flourish readily, while another struggles desperately against great odds? Unfortunately, we don't always know. But we do know that stresses to marriage provide tests to which we must respond. And as we respond in faithfulness, God will build our character.

Notes

Chapter 1: A Positive Vision of Marriage
[1]David Olson, Hamilton I. McCubbin, Howard Barnes, Andrea Larsen, Marla Muxen and Marc Wilson, *Families: What Makes Them Work* (Beverly Hills, Calif.: Sage, 1983).
[2]Gayla Margolin, "Behavior Exchange in Happy and Unhappy Marriages: A Family Cycle Perspective," *Behavior Therapy* 12 (1981):329-43.
[3]Bernard I. Murstein, *Paths to Marriage* (Beverly Hills, Calif.: Sage, 1986).

Chapter 2: The Blurred Vision
[1]Charles R. Figley, "Catastrophes: An Overview of Family Reactions," in *Stress and the Family*, vol. 2, *Coping with Catastrophe*, ed. Charles R. Figley and Hamilton I. McCubbin (New York: Brunner/Mazel, 1983), 6.
[2]Patricia Noller, *Nonverbal Communication and Marital Interaction* (Oxford, U.K.: Pergamon Press, 1984).
[3]Arnold A. Lazarus, *Marital Myths* (San Luis Obispo, Calif.: Impact, 1985); Aaron T. Beck, *Love Is Never Enough* (New York: Harper & Row, 1988).

Chapter 4: Bringing the Vision into Focus
[1]Alan S. Gurman and David P. Kniskern, "Family Therapy Outcome Research: Knowns and Unknowns," in *Handbook of Family Therapy* (New York: Brunner/Mazel, 1981). This finding has been questioned by Richard A. Wells and Vincent J. Gianetti, "Individual Marital Therapy: A Critical Reappraisal," *Family Process* 25 (1986):43-51.
[2]Everett L. Worthington Jr., Beverley G. Buston and T. Michael Hammonds, "A Component Analysis of Marriage Enrichment: Information and Treatment Modality," *Journal of Counseling and Development* 67 (1989):555-60.
[3]William J. Doherty, Mary Ellen Lester and Geoffrey Leigh, "Marriage Encounter Weekends: Couples Who Win and Couples Who Lose," *Journal of Marital and Family Therapy* 12 (1986):49-61; William J. Doherty and B. Walker, "Marriage Encounter Casualties: A Preliminary Investigation," *American Journal of Family Therapy* 10 (1982):10-25.

Chapter 5: Preparing to Change
[1]Frank Peretti, *This Present Darkness* (Westchester, Ill.: Crossway Books, 1986), and *Piercing the Darkness* (Westchester, Ill.: Crossway Books, 1989).

Chapter 7: Closeness
[1]Larry Christenson, "Paradoxes," audiotaped message to the 120 Fellowship, Berkeley, California, n.d.
[2]Mark T. Schaefer and David H. Olson, "Assessing Intimacy: The PAIR Inventory," *Journal of Marital and Family Therapy* 7 (1981):47-60.
[3]Richard B. Stuart, *Helping Couples Change: A Social Learning Approach to Marital Therapy* (New York: Guilford, 1980).
[4]Neil S. Jacobson and Gayla Margolin, *Marital Therapy: Strategies Based on Social Learning and Behavior Exchange Principles* (New York: Brunner/Mazel, 1979).
[5]Philip J. Guerin Jr., Leo F. Fay, Susan L. Burden and Judith Gilbert Kautto, *The Evaluation and Treatment of Marital Conflict: A Four-Stage Approach* (New York: Basic Books, 1987).
[6]Roger Fisher and William Ury, *Getting to Yes: Negotiating Agreement Without Giving In* (New York: Penguin Books, 1981).
[7]J. S. Annon, *Behavioral Treatment of Sexual Problems* (New York: Harper & Row, 1976).
[8]All suggestions for sex therapy may be found in Helen Singer Kaplan, *The Illustrated Manual of Sex Therapy,* 2d ed. (New York: Brunner/Mazel, 1987).

Chapter 8: Communication
[1]Lawrence Crabb Jr., *The Marriage Builder* (Grand Rapids, Mich.: Zondervan, 1982).
[2]Carol Tavris, *Anger: The Misunderstood Emotion* (New York: Simon & Schuster, 1982).
[3]Crabb, *Marriage Builder.*
[4]Norman Cousins, *Anatomy of an Illness As Perceived by the Patient: Reflections on Healing and Regeneration* (Toronto: Bantam Books, 1979).

Chapter 9: Resolving Conflict
[1]Jay Haley, *Problem Solving Therapy* (San Francisco: Jossey-Bass, 1978).
[2]John Gottman, Cliff Notarius, Jonni Gonso and Howard Markman, *A Couple's Guide to Communication* (Champaign, Ill.: Research Press, 1976).
[3]John Gottman, *Empirical Investigations of Marriage* (New York: Academic Press, 1979).
[4]Ibid.
[5]Eric Berne, *Games People Play* (New York: Grove, 1964).
[6]Robert P. Liberman, Eugenie G. Wheeler, Louis A. J. M. de Visser, Julie Kuehnel and Timothy Kuehnel, *Handbook of Marital Therapy: A Positive Approach to Helping Troubled Relationships* (New York: Plenum, 1980).
[7]Norman Wright, *Marital Counseling: A Biblical, Behavioral, Cognitive Approach* (New York: Harper & Row, 1981).
[8]Gottman et al., *Couple's Guide.*
[9]Fisher and Ury, *Getting to Yes.*

[10]Elizabeth Jones and Cynthia Gallois, "Spouses' Impressions of Rules for Communication in Public and Private Marital Conflicts," *Journal of Marriage and the Family* 51 (1989):957-67.

Chapter 10: Assigning and Accepting Responsibility

[1]Perry London, "Control in Psychotherapy," paper presented at the University of Missouri-Columbia, Winter 1977.

[2]Thomas N. Bradbury and Frank D. Fincham, "Attributions in Marriage: Review and Critique," *Psychological Bulletin* 107 (1990):3-33.

[3]Ulrich Neisser, *Cognition and Reality: Principles and Implications of Cognitive Psychology* (San Francisco: W. H. Freeman, 1976).

[4]Larry Christenson, *The Christian Family* (Minneapolis: Bethany Fellowship, 1970).

[5]Jay Haley and Cloe Madanes, "Strategic Marital Therapy: A Workshop for Treating Couples," workshop presented in Williamsburg, Va., October 1984.

Chapter 11: Commitment

[1]Malcolm Muggeridge, *A Third Testament* (1976; rpt. New York: Ballantine, 1983), 191-92.

[2]Ibid., 181.

[3]Caryl Rusbult, "A Longitudinal Test of the Investment Model: The Development (and Deterioriation) of Satisfaction and Commitment in Heterosexual Involvement," *Journal of Personality and Social Psychology* 45 (1983):101-17.

[4]Ellen Berscheid and Elaine Walster, *Interpersonal Attraction* (Reading, Mass.: Addison-Wesley, 1978).

[5]G. L. Clore and D. Byrne, "A Reinforcement-Affect Model of Attraction," in *Foundations of Interpersonal Attraction,* ed. T. L. Huston (New York: Academic Press, 1984), 143-70.

[6]Olson et al., *Families: What Makes Them Work.*

[7]Marilyn Machlowitz, *Workaholics: Living with Them, Working with Them* (Reading, Mass.: Addison-Wesley, 1980).

[8]Frank Pittman, *Private Lies: Infidelity and the Betrayal of Intimacy* (New York: W. W. Norton, 1989).

[9]Ibid.

[10]Frank Pittman, "What Price Camelot?" *Family Therapy Networker* 13 (May/June 1989):20-30.

[11]Ibid.

[12]Ibid.